Fifty-Fifty

Contemplating Life's Journey at Middle Age

Mark Kelland

ISBN: 1460988914
ISBN-13: 978-1460988916

Dedication

to Blue, Meow, Shep, Bulldog, Banshee, Rat Patrol, and Sunny

true friends through thick and thin

fyi: dog, cat, dog, horse, cat, cat, dog; in that order

Sunny striking a fine pose.

Table of Contents

Acknowledgements

There are certain people who have had an influence on my whole life in ways they probably never knew: Billy Graham (a police officer and boxing/wrestling instructor from Foxborough, MA, *not* the famous preacher), Bill O'Reilly (a pharmacist and father-figure from Foxborough, MA, *definitely not* the other guy), Arthur Sullivan, Dr. Alice Young, Arthur Niemoller, and Mark D. Kelland, Jr. In a similar way, there are some very special martial arts instructors who provided me with a background for working with people who have physical disabilities: Shawn and Andrea Withers (true masters as far as I am concerned), Grandmaster Mark Shuey, Sr., and Master Jurgen Schmidt.

I would like to thank everyone at Magic Brazilian Jiu Jitsu for providing a wonderful environment for me to continue my martial arts training and safely learn some new styles. Brazilian Jiu Jitsu and Muay Thai are great! Special thanks to Mike, Randy, Mary, Doug, Corey, Travis, and co-owners Amy and Matt.

Special thanks to Mary Ann Fogal and Corey Ottgen for reading this book and providing me with their comments., and to Megan Ottgen for the photo on page 84.

Preface

The candle burns soft,
Souls awaken with each breath,
God is silent with us.

I wrote this haiku on a silent retreat led by Fr. Laurence Freeman, Director of the World Community for Christian Meditation. I wrote the poem on Pentecost, during meditation. I guess I wasn't really meditating yet, but I'd had a wonderful meditation earlier in the day, and again afterward. As I prepared myself to meditate, I kept my eyes open and focused on the candle flame. The poem came to me very quickly, and then I settled into a very pleasing meditation. It was Sunday, May 15, 2005, in the evening.

At this particular moment I am just a few days away from May, 2010. I can hardly believe the extraordinary changes that have occurred in my life over the past five years. Some have been wonderful, some have been agonizing. I have developed new hope for the future, and a vision for doing good things with my life. I very nearly committed suicide, and depression continues to plague me. Turning 50 years old can be a depressing milestone for anyone, but I have lost a little more than my identity as a young man.

I lost my wife and best friend. She decided to take her life in a different direction. I lost both of my hips to an old injury, and now the titanium and chromium that have taken their places set off metal detectors. I have not fully recovered, and I doubt I will. I lost my first son yet again. This was the year he would have turned 18. Each major milestone that he never reached brings pain and sadness to the surface of my being yet again.

So, have I become a lonely, depressed, physically disabled, old man? Perhaps even something less of a man? Actually, I have also gained a few good things: some knowledge, some wisdom, and the awareness of a path that one would be well-advised to follow. Some would say I am already following that path; maybe I am. But if I were, life would be good. Instead, life continues to be a challenge. That is what this book is about.

I have written many professional articles, and a couple of books (including a college textbook, an extraordinary chore I will never tackle again). While writing this book I am going to relax. I may cite a few references, or not. I guess we'll see. What I really want to do is just write the book, and take even the academic material for granted, as if all the information were common knowledge. Of course, it is only common knowledge to those who know it. For everyone else, I will leave it to you to do your own research, to discover your own path toward new and interesting bits of wisdom.

Mark Kelland, April, 2010

Introduction

People are fascinating, and some lead very interesting lives. I like to think that my life has been more interesting than most, but maybe I'm just good at convincing myself of that. I used to say that I didn't mind being called anything, good or bad, just so long as I wasn't called boring.

As I prepared to collect these thoughts, some of which were jotted down over the past year, I realized three important things. I have made one great mistake in my life - her name is Donna. I made one critically good decision, which likely changed the course of my entire life - I allowed a detective from the District 2 police station in Boston to arrest me over the telephone. And the best news I ever received was my son's autopsy. Each of these little bits of information cries out for explanation, but you'll have to wait for that (or try flipping ahead, something I just had to do with the final Harry Potter novel!).

Life seldom proceeds according to our plans. Sometimes the changes might have been predictable, if we simply kept our eyes open to the things our families and friends have experienced. Other times the changes are more dramatic, sometimes tragic, and those moments can truly challenge us. Some people rise to the occasion and grow from their experiences; others crumble in the face of adversity and become lesser for it. The ones who cannot adapt to the real challenges may be doomed to live a meaningless life, to lose sight of all that life is about, and all that life has to offer. But this raises a most difficult question: What is life all about?

The meaning of life is unique to each individual. But what really matters is that there must be some *meaning* to it. Without meaning in our lives, we stop living. The existential psychoanalyst Viktor Frankl, who spent several years in Nazi concentration camps, saw that the people who clung to meaning in their lives, even while enduring the horrors of the death camps, were able to survive. Those who lost any sense of meaning lost all hope, and soon wasted away and died. The need for our life to have purpose seems to be nearly as important as our ability to breathe. So let's take a brief look at what used to provide meaning in my life.

In roughly this order, I used to identify my life with my family, my career, my home, and the desire to create some sort of legacy. I married a wonderful woman, after the death of our first son we had two more great children, we built a home in Hartland, MI, and I became active in community service and wrote a college level personality textbook. Doing pretty darn good so far, right? Guess again!

I had originally planned to write much of this book in the form of a journal. I should have been more realistic. Every time I start a journal, it quickly comes to an end. On some special trips I have been able to keep a journal, such as when my brother-in-law and I hiked the Appalachian Trail through Shenandoah National Park one week, or when I spent a week taking a mountaineering course on Mt. Rainier in Washington. But as for a general journal on my daily life, I just can't seem to do it. I tried once again to start one on my 50th birthday, so I would like to share that entry:

> _February 6, 2009:_ So far it has been a bad day. I got into a nasty fight with my wife and my son John. John and I get into fights on occasion. He is 12 years old, and has a very high-strung temperament, which he clearly gets from me. So when we clash, it usually isn't pretty. It's especially problematic when my wife intervenes, which she is prone to do when the kids and I get into it. She always takes their side, and they know it. When parents disagree with each other, and take sides, the kids know it and use it against whoever they are most upset with. This is one of the main reasons my wife wants a divorce. If we could afford it, I'm sure she would have left already.
>
> When something like this happens, it's usually just another bad day. But today is a little bit different. Today I am 50 years old. That partially explains the first half of the title. I say it only partially explains it because I actually have three distinct meanings for fifty-fifty. First, I am fifty years old, and I would like to lose 50 pounds. There's another reason my wife wants a divorce (the 50 pounds that is, I don't think she minds that I am 50 years old). As I write this book, it will partly be a journal. The journal portion will focus on my efforts to lose the weight and get back in shape. It's not that I am very obese, at least I don't think I am. I exercise, I practice Taekwondo, I do things outdoors like fishing and taking the dog for hikes in the local state park. But I also like to eat too much, and as I have already mentioned, I'm not young anymore. So I agree that I need to lose some weight, and maybe this time I'm serious about it. Don't we all know what that's like?

I am now divorced, and I struggle to have a good relationship with my teenage boys. I'll write more about family in a later chapter. Even though my ex-wife doesn't really want our house, which I still think of as our home, she wanted the kids. I wanted the kids to stay in their home. So now I live in a small apartment, while still paying half the mortgage on the house. So, there goes what I thought was the meaning in my life associated with family and home. As for community service and my career, it suddenly didn't seem very important without the things I cared for so much more. Nonetheless, as Frankl observed long ago, we need to find meaning in our lives. So I have been working hard to accept my life as it is, and to develop other sources of meaning. I haven't given up on the kids, of course, and I am supposed to get the house back in a couple of years. So, if I can just ride this out, it may all work out in the end. The most important part of the plan is that I must not bet everything on any one specific outcome, especially an outcome beyond my control.

* * *

As mentioned above, the first meaning of the title *Fifty-Fifty* refers to my age and my weight. But there are a couple of other ways in which I want to consider the meaning of the title. According to ancient Vedic tradition, the ideal life proceeds through four stages. Each stage is 25 years, and the first two stages are all about the business of life. The enigmatic psychiatrist Carl Jung called this first half of life the biological period. At the age of 50, the official date of midlife, you began what Jung called the cultural period of life. According to the Vedic tradition, these later stages of life involve increasingly focusing on what matters most in life: your relationship with God. For Jung, these latter stages were about creating one's legacy. This was a time in life when a person should have the freedom to do things for others, and to contribute to society in meaningful ways.

Having recently turned 50 years old, I am right at this point of transition between focusing on the business of life (education, family, establishing a career, etc.) and turning toward making a contribution to life and to my community (community service, scholarship, mentorship, etc.). As important as family and a sense of having a "home" may be, there is clearly a great deal of meaning still to be found in my life. Most importantly, I can't control my family situation, but I can control whether or not I choose to do my best in contributing to society. Hopefully I will set a good example for my children, and my whole life will fall into place. Only time will tell.

In this book I also plan to pay some attention to a third meaning of fifty-fifty. This would be the most common use of the term: life is a crap-shoot. You take the good with the bad. Some things work out, others don't. You can't really predict much of anything. The odds of life working out the way you want are just fifty-fifty. However, it is a choice whether we consider misfortune to be anything other than just normal life. It is a choice whether we are troubled by those things that interfere with our desires and expectations. And most importantly, it is entirely up to us whether we even have desires or expectation, or how those desires and expectations affect us.

Let me say right now, at the beginning, that I am not really that well adjusted. I am not at peace with myself or with life in general. But I am trying. And now that I have learned a lot in life, I hope to truly focus on putting it into practice. I hope that by sharing these reflections on what I have learned and what I am experiencing having just passed my 50th birthday, that I may provide some food for thought for others who have, are, or will be experiencing something similar.

The Ancient Vedas and Carl Jung

Some 5,000 years ago, in ancient India, the Vedas were first written down. I couldn't begin to describe everything in these extraordinary works, but one thing stands out for me: they describe an ideal life pattern. According to the Vedas, an ideal life proceeds through four stages: student, householder, forest dweller, and renunciant (or wandering ascetic). Each stage lasts 25 years. At the completion of one's life, if all has gone well, the person will have become enlightened. If they have not achieved enlightenment, but they have led a good life, they will be reincarnated in the next life with conditions more favorable to successfully achieving enlightenment in that life.

The student must learn the important lessons necessary for living a life in which one can contribute to the functioning of society. They need an education, and religious/spiritual education is an important aspect of the overall education. In addition to reading, writing, and arithmetic (as well as literature, science, history, languages, etc.), they would study Yoga. Yoga means "yoke" or "union," and it refers to union with God. Yoga is much more than just the stretching exercises (or *asanas*) that constitute part of Hatha Yoga. It is a way of settling the mind, so that we can set aside all of our worldly connections and distractions, leaving only an awareness of that spark of divinity within us that is life itself. You can call it a soul if you wish, that's as good a term as any. An important aspect of Yoga is meditation. So although the student would be studying many things about the world and the functioning of society in terms of daily life, they would also learn to meditate, clear their mind of those worldly thoughts, and be one with the God who created everything and who gives us life.

The householder is very much what the name implies. After growing up and becoming prepared to contribute to society, you do just that. You build a home and start a family. You establish a career in order to support that family. You raise your children, and help them to grow and learn and prepare to be the next generation of householders. This can be a busy and difficult time. You are not supposed to forget about your relationship with God, certainly you would want to set a good example for your children. But again, it is a busy time. The pressures of earning an income, fixing things around the house, keeping track of the children and keeping them safe (especially the little ones), all keep our minds full of too many thoughts and concerns.

* * *

At life's midpoint, according to this tradition, our oldest children are ready to become householders themselves. That allows us the freedom to become a forest dweller. We can build a little hut by the edge of the village, near the forest, and begin to practice our Yoga once again. We are still available to our children and our new grandchildren. We help to raise and educate them. We are still available to help with the family business, or with their fledgling careers. Yet we turn over most of the responsibilities in life to them, and we have time for ourselves. Now, at this point I feel the need to remind you that this is an old philosophy. Very few of us still live in villages, fewer still follow in the footsteps of their parents in terms of choosing a career, let alone take over a family business. Shortly we will see a more modern perspective offered by Carl Jung, and that should help clarify how this perspective on the ideal pattern of life can still be applied in the world today.

Finally, the individual reaches the point of become a renunciant. They renounce all worldly connections, and begin to immerse themselves in the practice of Yoga. They may even leave their home and become a wandering ascetic. Once again, it is hard to imagine this happening in our society today, at least the wandering ascetic aspect of it, but a person can certainly become deeply spiritual in a healthy sense, should they make that choice. And making that choice is very important, because the end of this final stage is clear and inevitable: we all die eventually. There are certainly people who believe that we simply blink out of existence when we die, but most of us don't believe that. We have many different beliefs about what happens after death, and questions about what it will be like, but nonetheless, most of us believe there is something beyond this existence.

* * *

The fields of psychology and psychiatry have largely ignored spirituality. The great psychoanalyst Sigmund Freud despised religion, and blamed many of the world's problems on it. He went so far as to say that when the great masses of people learn that there is no God they will rebel and begin acting out their unconscious id impulses. Freud, however, still recognized that religion was a major factor in many people's lives. Being Jewish, as were most of the early psychoanalysts, Freud was concerned that psychoanalysis would be viewed as a Jewish science, and there was a great deal of prejudice toward and discrimination against Jews in Europe in the early 1900s. Thus, Freud was thrilled when the renowned psychiatrist Eugen Bleuler sent his top assistant to study psychoanalysis with Freud. The assistant's name was Carl Jung. Jung was young, intelligent, visionary, and Christian. Freud and Jung became very close for a few years, but Jung had radical ideas of his own. Jung had radical, *spiritual* ideas. Indeed, according to

Jung, God himself had told Jung in a vision not to ever follow the rules of other men. So Jung and Freud parted ways. This had a profound personal effect on Jung, whose father had died while he was in college, but it also freed Jung to pursue those ideas that seemed so radical.

There are two particular concepts proposed by Jung that I would like to discuss. First, the collective unconscious, and second, personality development in adulthood (which will bring us back the life pattern proposed in the Vedas).

* * *

Jung's father was a scholar of Asian languages. As a child, Jung enjoyed learning about the Hindu religion, particularly the many animal gods (such as Hanuman, the monkey god, and Ganesh, the elephant-headed god). Jung agreed with Freud that we have an unconscious mind, but he split it into two parts: the personal unconscious and the collective unconscious. According to Jung, all people and all cultures share essentially the same collective unconscious. How is this possible? Reincarnation! If we have all lived countless lives in the past, we will all have experienced the wide variety of cultures and environments that the world has to offer. Thus, it seems as if we have the same collective unconscious, because each of us has experienced all that life has had to offer throughout the evolution of the human species.

Since most Americans have a Christian religious tradition, the idea of reincarnation is a problem for many of my students. Most Christians will tell you that Christians don't believe in reincarnation. Unfortunately, that doesn't agree with what Jesus of Nazareth had to say in the gospels. Particularly in the gospel of Matthew, Jesus clearly states that John the Baptist is the reincarnation of the prophet Elijah, who was sent to herald the coming of the Messiah (who Christians believe is Jesus Christ). There is another interesting story, in the gospel of John, where a man who was born blind is brought to Jesus for help. Jesus' disciples ask who sinned, the blind man or his parents, that he was born blind. Well, if the man was born blind because he had sinned, he must have done so in a previous life, and was then suffering the consequences of his bad karma! So it appears that Jesus' own disciples at least considered reincarnation to be possible, and of course they should have, since John the Baptist was Elijah reincarnated. Now these examples by no means suggest that reincarnation is a common occurrence. Indeed, Jesus said that John the Baptist was the greatest man who ever lived, and the blind man was not blind because of any sin at all. Nonetheless, according to gospel, reincarnation is possible (of course, it goes without saying, God can do anything!). And that is something Jung had in mind as he considered the nature of the collective unconscious.

The second radical difference between Jung and Freud, the one which takes us back to the Vedic stages of life, has to do with personality development in adulthood. Freud considered personality to be largely set in stone by the age of five years old. Jung agreed that early childhood was very important, but he also believed that adulthood became more important. Jung simplified the Vedic stages of life by combining the first two stages (student and householder) into what he called the biological stage of life. During this first half of life, we go about the business of continuing human existence. We prepare ourselves for adulthood, and then as adults we have and raise children, and we contribute to the continuity of our community through our careers and friendships. This is an important time, but not the most important.

Jung then combined the latter two stages of life (forest dweller and renunciant) into the cultural period of life. Having become established, and having turned over many of life's basic responsibilities to a younger generation, we now have both the means and the time to contribute to society in significant and meaningful ways. And when we make significant contributions to our society, helping to make life better for others, we are likely to improve our standing with whatever cosmic force(s) you believe in. We are either doing Christ's work on earth, or creating good Karma, or simply being a moral and ethical humanist (not that being moral and ethical is simple!), etc.

What makes Jung's theory on the importance of the cultural period in life of particular interest to me is timing. According to some authors, each stage in the Vedic life pattern is 25 years. Thus, Jung's cultural stage should begin at the age of 50. I turned 50 a year ago, so I am right at the beginning of the cultural stage of life. The main purpose of this book is to share with you how my life has approached this very important time, and what my thoughts and plans are for actively pursuing meaningful goals that will make worthwhile cultural contributions.

There is, however, a problem. I am depressed. I have suffered from depression most of my life. Quite recently, my wife of 23 years left me. The divorce also led to some difficult financial problems. I am physically disabled, due to an old injury I received when I was crushed by a horse (not the horse mentioned in the acknowledgements, but my horse was friends with the other horse). So, it is not easy for me to make plans for a bright, meaningful, and fulfilling future, despite the many good things in my life. As I often tell my students, you cannot apply logic to abnormal psychology. You cannot add up the good things, weigh them against the bad things, throw in some hopeful philosophy, and then simply say "See, the sum total of the numbers tells us you should be happy!"

So, I will be sharing stories about my life that I imagine many of you will be able to understand within the context of your own life. There is good, and there is bad. Hopefully we can cope with the bad, enjoy the good, and keep muddling along through this thing called life. But it need not be a bleak prospect. There are a few hopeful, spiritual, philosophies out there which offer us help and guidance. Depending on who you are as a person, I would not advocate one over another. Instead, I will talk about a blending of philosophies that is proving helpful in my own life. You will need to pursue your own path. For me, at least for the moment, I am practicing Buddhist mindfulness and equanimity, and blending it with self-actualization and humanistic psychology as taught by Carl Rogers and Abraham Maslow.

* * *

Jung was also very interested in symbolism. Sometimes, we seem to recognize symbolic power in a relationship between seemingly unrelated events. If there is a meaningful coincidence between an event outside of ourselves and the psychological impact within ourselves, it seems as if the coincidence is anything but. Might a higher power have caused such events to coincide for a reason? Jung referred to the meaningful connection between those events as synchronicity.

I have had some very powerful synchronicity events in my life, and I find it very difficult to dismiss them as mere coincidence. As such, they were deeply meaningful, spiritual moments, which helped to shape my life.

* * *

In February, 1992, our first son, Mark David Kelland, Jr., died at birth. Later that year, I was traveling across the country, taking a whole week to get to a neuroscience convention in California, and I decided to hike up Wheeler Peak, the highest point in New Mexico (13,161 feet). I arrived a little late in the day, but decided I had enough time to make the climb and get back down off the ridge before dark. I just made it, but still had a few miles to go on the jeep trail down to the parking lot. Along the way, I stopped and looked back up at Wheeler Peak. I turned off my flashlight, and in the dark I could just make out the outline of the mountain against the night sky. I prayed to God for a sign that our son was in heaven. The instant I said "Amen," a brilliant shooting star streaked across the sky and descended behind Wheeler Peak! I took it to be the sign I had asked for.

* * *

When I was growing up, we lived next door to Bill and Jackie O'Reilly, who co-owned the corner drugstore in the center of town. When I was young I mowed their lawn in the summer and shoveled the snow from their driveway in the winter. Following the blizzard of 1978 I stood on the roof of Bill O'Reilly's car shoveling waist-deep snow. When I was old enough to get a regular job, I asked Mr. O'Reilly for a letter of recommendation for a job at the local newspaper. He declined, saying he wanted me to work at their drugstore. But he didn't say anything else, until Mrs. O'Reilly told him to give me a job. So, I worked at the drugstore from the age of 15 to 20 years old. I even began college at the same school they had attended: the Massachusetts College of Pharmacy. Although I changed schools and switched my major to psychology, I was always hopeful that the O'Reilly's would be proud of me. Unfortunately, Bill O'Reilly died a week after I graduated from college. Jackie O'Reilly eventually retired and sold their building, and the old corner drugstore in the center of town ceased to exist.

Eventually I moved away, pursued my career in psychology, got married and had children, and visits to Massachusetts became few and far between. One night, about 25 years after I had worked at the drugstore, I had a very vivid and moving dream. I was standing in the center of Foxborough, MA, looking at the building where the drugstore had been. I was overwhelmed by a profound sense of sadness, sad that things must change with time and cannot remain the same, no matter how much we may long for the past. I awoke from that dream astonished by its sense of reality and its emotional impact. The next morning my mother called me, and told me that Jackie O'Reilly had died during the night! Was it merely a coincidence that I dreamt about O'Reilly's Pharmacy and felt the sadness of seeing time pass away, while Jackie O'Reilly was in reality passing away, or was it something more? There can be no scientific explanation. I searched my mind for anything that might have coincidentally caused me to think about the drugstore the day before, but nothing came to mind. And yet there was an alternative explanation, one that was not at all scientific. Had Jackie O'Reilly's spirit passed by and said goodbye, on her way to the great beyond?

Religion and Psychology

As mentioned above, psychiatry and psychology have long avoided the study of religion and spirituality, due in part to Sigmund Freud despising religion. Having been raised Jewish, Freud's last book was a very convincing linguistic/archeological analysis of the story of Moses. Freud concluded that Moses was actually an Egyptian, that the monotheistic religion was Egyptian, and that the entire Jewish faith was just a myth. This was pretty heavy stuff for someone of Jewish descent to write. Instead, Freud put his faith in the science of psychoanalysis (though few others considered psychoanalysis to be scientific).

Today, there is growing interest in the roles of religion and spirituality in people's lives; and to the extent that they are a significant part of many people's lives, they must be part of psychology. Likewise, there have been many notable psychiatrists and psychologists whose faith was an important aspect of their theories. But first, let's consider the difference between religion and spirituality. Religion generally refers to doctrine, or to use the somewhat less pleasant word, dogma. These are rules made by people, though they typically claim to have been divinely inspired. Spirituality, on the other hand, refers more to one's personal sense of faith, the belief that there is something greater than the physics and probabilities of the creation of the universe from a big bang, through geologic time and evolution, to where we are today muddling about this water and oxygen covered rock. People who are religious tend to associate closely with their church, and exclude people of other religions. People who are spiritual are more likely to be open minded, and to admire a variety of different faiths. I realize this is a very general characterization, but there is definitely some truth to it.

* * *

So where do I stand? I am a religious pluralist. I was baptized in a Presbyterian church, a fairly mainstream Christian faith. I was confirmed in a Congregationalist church, again fairly mainstream Christian. At the age of thirty I became Roman Catholic, largely because I was very impressed by the faith and active involvement of my wife's family, but also because I care deeply about the Sacraments of Reconciliation and Communion (and had cared about them since I was a little child). Having spent 8 years as a full-time, biomedical research scientist, spending each day doing surgery and administering a variety of experimental drugs and chemicals, while studying theories related to schizophrenia, Parkinson's disease, and Tourette Syndrome, I came to a surprising conclusion. The more we learn about the brain, the mind, biology, neuroscience, etc., the farther we are from really understanding *life!* The true nature of life itself simply cannot be found in the biochemical machinery of cellular organisms. There must be something more. And that something must be God. Unfortunately, the Roman Catholic Church was not the right place for me to continue my search for an understanding of God's plan for my life.

First, the sex abuse scandal that has rocked the Roman Catholic Church became common knowledge. Second, Cardinal Ratzinger was elected as Pope Benedict XVI. The problem arising from the first event seems simple enough as a moral issue, but why the concern regarding this particular pope? I believe he is a truly evil man. He served in the Hitler youth. He has openly condemned Islam and other faiths. I don't buy the lame excuses he and the Vatican have put forth. He left the Hitler youth only weeks before the fall of Nazi Germany, and since he quoted a 500 year old document when condemning Islam how can he claim it was taken out of context? Worst of all, however, is that he personally protected a pedophile priest when the local bishop asked to have the priest removed. Now that he is being sued by some of the abuse victims, he is claiming diplomatic immunity as a head-of-state. Jesus didn't hide from the Sanhedrin or from Pontius Pilate. Perhaps the pope should considering following the example of Jesus Christ and answer for his sins! Unlike Jesus Christ, Pope Benedict XVI seems to have quite a few to answer for, not the least of which is that ridiculous pair of red Prada shoes. Can the man look any more like the Devil in some of those pictures?

* * *

As I became interested in Eastern philosophies, particularly traditional Yoga, Buddhism, and Taoism, I moved rapidly toward being a religious pluralist. The Buddhist concept of non-attachment helped me to separate the bad things in the church from the things that were important to me. I also became interested in some authors who advocate a pluralistic view of religion. One author I really enjoy is Anthony De Mello, a Jesuit priest from India (who died in 1987). I am also very interested in the work of Fr. Peter Phan, a Vietnamese Catholic priest. Both of these men are Roman Catholic Christians who recognize the valuable spiritual history and lessons of Yoga and Buddhism. They have also both been condemned by the Vatican for their views (I believe De Mello was condemned by Cardinal Ratzinger himself when he was the so-called defender of the faith, and Phan was condemned by Ratzinger's successor in that position). It is quite interesting to me that no Buddhists I know of have condemned Thich Nhat Hanh for speaking most highly of Christianity and the Roman Catholic church.

* * *

12

But enough of my own issues for a moment; let's get back to psychology and religion. An interesting movement which is rapidly gaining strength is the field of positive psychology. Positive psychologists study such things as well-being and human virtue. Like any complex human factor, religion and spirituality are neither good nor bad. There is good religion and bad religion. There is good spirituality and bad spirituality. What is most important is whether one's religious or spiritual faith serves to better one's life and the lives of others. When this is the case, religion and spirituality appear to be beneficial for the human condition. As one part of a broader spectrum of topics, positive psychology examines the good that religion and spirituality can provide.

Although there are a variety of ways that one can study and/or practice spirituality within a psychological context, there is an Eastern philosophy that presents an intriguing case. Strictly speaking, Buddhism is not a religion. It is, rather, a form of cognitive psychology. Gotama Buddha, who most people think of as *the* Buddha, didn't talk about the creation of the universe or what happens after we die. He talked about how we live our lives, and why human life inevitably leads to suffering. Gotama Buddha realized the Four Noble Truths: human life is suffering, we suffer because of our cravings, if we would stop craving we would stop suffering, and there is a way to stop the craving known as the Eight-Fold Path or the Middle Way. Anyone familiar with cognitive psychology will recognize the basic principles here – that we create our own suffering and we could simply stop it if we really wanted to. But putting an end to our suffering seldom proves to be a simple task.

* * *

I consider it important to bring spirituality into my psychology classes because it just doesn't seem good enough to treat psychology as a science. Yes, much of the work done in the field of psychology is scientific; the biomedical research I have published is some pretty serious stuff. I spent day after day for eight years doing surgery and testing experimental drugs on rats, studying Tourette Syndrome, Parkinson's disease and schizophrenia. In some of my current classes I use physiological recording equipment to measure electroencephalography (brain waves), heart rate, and muscle activity. However, as important as the scientific method is for moving psychology beyond our expectations regarding human behavior, if we lose sight of how fascinating each person truly is we have lost something precious.

Psychological theories need to be tested; we often make the wrong predictions. For example, Stanley Milgram was told by many so-called experts that virtually no subjects would complete his study on obedience in which the subject thought they might seriously injure or kill another person.

13

However, they nearly all did (for those in the primary test group). Although many people use Milgram's experiment as an example of unethical research, Milgram was actually ahead of his time in terms of his ethical concerns. His research proved to be most valuable, he debriefed subjects and offered follow-up care. He complied with most of today's primary ethical guidelines long before such ethical guidelines existed. And yet, the expert predictions regarding his results were almost entirely wrong. So we need controlled research studies. But if we rely solely on scientific research, we miss out on the other side of human life, the mysterious and spiritual aspects.

* * *

When I teach psychology classes there are often occasions when we have the opportunity to discussion religion and spirituality. Many students find this refreshing, and others find it offensive. The difference is usually based on being open-minded. Students who are open-minded enjoy discussing complex and even controversial topics. We don't always agree, but nothing makes me happier than having a well-informed student offer a thoughtful argument against my point of view. That is the point at which we all begin to really learn something new and valuable.

In contrast, some students are closed-minded. They know very little, and they don't want to be told anything else. Why would you go to college with the intent of remaining ignorant? I don't ever want to change anyone's beliefs. What I want them to do is look deeply into the truth of what they believe and then make choices which benefit both themselves and others. When they do that, we typically find ourselves on common ground. In other words, I want my students to think in ways which emulate the behavior of treating others as you would like to have others treat you. Love your neighbor, in both action and thought!

* * *

Shortly before the new millennium, Martin Seligman, then president of the American Psychological Association, urged psychologists to rediscover their forgotten mission to encourage the growth of human strengths and virtues. He called this new area positive psychology. The goal of positive psychology is to find ways in which psychologists can help people be happier and lead more fulfilling lives, and as a field of study it is providing a focal point for psychologists to become more appreciative of human nature.

The study of virtue is hardly new. Gotama Buddha emphasized the importance of virtue some 2,500 years ago. In a previous book, I noted the close correspondence between ancient martial arts codes of conduct and the six core virtues identified by Seligman and his colleague Christopher Peterson.

Those core virtues are wisdom and knowledge, courage, humanity, justice, temperance, and transcendence. Transcendence includes within it the character strength of spirituality.

* * *

Spirituality appears to have emerged consistently across cultures throughout the history of humanity, and as such, it appears to be an essential attribute of human nature. A belief in the supernatural may well be a natural consequence of child development, based on a sense of awe regarding how incredible parents seem to be and how vast the world appears to the eyes of a young child. This natural tendency to seek spiritual or magical explanations for the extraordinary world that children experience is likely the reason that religion and religious ritual are cultural universals. William James, America's foremost psychologist, wrote extensively on religious and spiritual pursuits. Though the study of spirituality was largely suppressed in the early days of psychology and psychiatry, the recent growth of positive psychology has rekindled an interest. Indeed, individuals who are spiritually active tend to have higher levels of well-being. And even some atheist psychotherapists have acknowledged that if their patients are religious, then psychotherapy must incorporate a spiritual aspect in order to be effective.

Positive psychology may be a new field, but positive approaches have been around for a while, most notably among the humanistic and existential psychologists. Carl Rogers and Abraham Maslow emphasized self-actualization, the fulfillment of human potential, and Maslow included within it the so-called "oceanic feeling" that comes with peak experiences. Maslow believed that this sense of oneness with life was the basis for what was interpreted by early humans as the presence and/or voice of God (such as when God speaks to prophets). Maslow's famous hierarchy of needs begins with four deficiency needs: physiological (e.g., food, water, air), safety, belonging, and esteem needs. At the top of the hierarchy is the one being need of self-actualization.

Thus, as easy as it may be to just muddle through life in relatively good times, when faced with a real life-threatening challenge, the sense of meaning in one's life that may arise through a spiritual foundation can actually be essential for life itself. Of course, one can find meaning in things which are not spiritual. But does such meaning continue when one has lost everything? That is when one's faith becomes most important, and faith is only strong when it is faith in something that cannot be challenged or taken away.

* * *

As part of studying the unconscious, and in consideration of his own personal interests, Carl Jung often consulted the ancient Chinese oracle known as the *I Ching* (the *Book of Changes*). Jung also made use of this oracle to examine his theory of synchronicity. Once in a while I consult the *I Ching* myself, and it always proves to be fascinating. I know how to debunk pseudo-science, astrology, fortune-telling, etc., and it would be easy to dismiss the *I Ching* as nothing more than just another fortune-telling book. However, it seems to offer such compelling reflection that I have a hard time dismissing its value. Perhaps the key is in triggering our own true thoughts and feelings, even those buried in our unconscious minds. The whole process of psychoanalysis is meant to bring our unconscious conflicts out into the open, where we can then deal with them. If that is what the *I Ching* does, so be it. Let me share my recent experience with you, and you can judge for yourself.

I was very nearly done with this book, but I wasn't sure whether or not I was at all happy with it. I was finishing this chapter last, as I often write things out of order, or add to them later, and given this topic I decided to consult the *I Ching*. Following the standard procedure, I received the hexagram *chun* (difficulty at the beginning). *Chun* suggests that a period of great difficulty is before you, but that if you are patient and embrace nonaction, you will achieve success. *Chun* encourages you to experience your suffering, don't avoid it, things will work out in the end (the translation I use is by Brian Browne Walker, 1992, St. Martin's Press).

Even more interesting is that when consulting the *I Ching* there is more than one way to get the primary hexagram. Based on how you obtain it, some lines can change, and that leads to a secondary hexagram. But I got *chun* without any changing lines, so I was "told" to accept my suffering, be patient, wait for better times to come about as a result of my nonaction, and nothing else! I am very good at the defense mechanism of rationalization. If I'd had a secondary hexagram, I might have justified any possibility of not accepting things as they are, I might have justified blaming others or feeling sorry for myself. But I had no secondary hexagram. Knowing myself, I believe the *I Ching* was right in giving me simple, clear, and direct counsel.

Buddhist Non-Attachment and the Humanistic Psychology of Carl Rogers and Abraham Maslow

Buddhism is not a religion *per se*. It's really a philosophy of how to live one's live, a cognitive psychological approach to making life better, though it does address major humanistic and existential questions. Perhaps what attracts me most to Buddhism is its focus on compassion. Compassion is the ideal Buddhist emotional state, and the Dalai Lama has written some wonderful books on this topic. When we try to align our lives with caring about other people, with caring about the conditions of their lives, regardless of how situations have arisen in their current state, we can begin to accept both ourselves and others without judgment or condemnation. We can also begin the most important step in changing the world for the better, and that is, changing ourselves for the better.

* * *

Gotama Buddha came to realize what he taught as the Four Noble Truths. First, human life is suffering. Second, we suffer because of our desires, or our craving. Third, if we stopped craving things, we would no longer suffer. And finally, there is a way to end our craving: the Middle Way, or the Eightfold Path (right knowledge, right intention, right speech, right conduct, right livelihood, right effort, right mindfulness, and right concentration).

The first two noble truths are a profound insight. We are never satisfied. If we take a bite of something delicious, we want more. If you find a dollar on the street, do you look around for more? When you are in love, do you feel an intense desire to spend more time with that person? We always want *more*. This is the beginning of cognitive therapy, to realize that we are creating our own misfortune. If we could simply accept the good things in life without being attached to them, without *needing* them, then we would no longer suffer.

The Buddha told us how to do that: follow the Middle Way. Don't be a religious fanatic, following dogmatic rules and rituals. Likewise, don't irresponsibly attempt to satisfy every desire, through too much partying, drinking, illicit sex, etc. The Middle Way suggests a reasonable and balanced life. More specifically, the Buddha gave us eight key elements for finding this balance. Roughly speaking, when we understand the true nature of life and sincerely intend to become a better person, and we pursue a good life through our work and our relationships, and we then build on this base through

17

meditation and focus, we will no longer suffer. This is not the same thing as being happy, since happiness is still something that people desire. On the other hand, there is no reason for us to be unhappy, since escaping unhappiness is also something we desire. Rather, we should endeavor to neither seek happiness nor escape unhappiness. We need to simply accept life as it comes.

* * *

Different schools of Buddhism list different numbers of perfections. Be that as it may, at this point in my life I am focusing on the perfection of equanimity. Equanimity refers to a state in which all things are accepted equally, without judging whether they are "good" or "bad." In life, different things happen. Sometimes we like what happens, sometimes we don't. But the labels "good" and "bad" arise when we are attached to what has happened. We want more of the good things, and we want to avoid the bad things. What if we simply accept things as they are?

There is nothing wrong with enjoying something we like, and if it leads to better conditions for us and for others, then it is OK. However, when we begin to crave more of anything, our behaviors change. Then, in accordance with the psychological principle of cognitive dissonance, our attitude follows our behavior. For example, we drink too much alcohol. We know it isn't good for us, but we rationalize it by saying something like "I had a really tough week at work, so I deserve to take a break." But how do we rationalize it if we wake up with a hangover the next day? Drinking too much alcohol is not good. Still, we don't have to then condemn ourselves for it. We just have to be mindful of our feelings, so that the next time we have a tough week at work we can make what the Buddhists call a skillful choice.

Likewise, suppose someone does something nasty to us. Do we seek revenge, or do we try to feel compassion for the conditions that led them to do this awful thing? I am not suggesting we let people take advantage of us, but how we react can be done skillfully, or not. When I have sincerely tried to put these principles into action, I have been amazed at how much better I felt afterward. The key is to be mindful of what you are thinking and feeling at the moment when the choice of how to react is being made.

* * *

So how do we prepare ourselves for being mindful of what we are about to do? Many people have at least a passing understanding of meditation, but mindfulness is something much more. It involves incorporating the practices of meditation into daily life, and then taking it to a higher level. Imagine watching your life as if you were another person. But it's not just watching your life from the outside. Imagine watching your life while having access to the four foundations of mindfulness: mindfulness of body, feelings, thoughts, and mental states. Now you are able to see how you react in detail, as well as knowing the psychological states of mind that exist within you and condition you to react in certain ways. Now you become able to make skillful choices before acting in ways you might later regret.

Meditation is not easy, and as something on a higher level, mindfulness is not easy at all. They take practice, and dedication. Meditation and mindfulness are skills that must be developed diligently. There are different types of meditation, and you may need to try several in order to find the one that is best for you. The great guru Paramahansa Yogananda teaches that it doesn't matter which type of meditation you prefer, just that you pick one and stay with it. I use a blend of Kriya Yoga, vipassana, and Zen no-thinking. I also take mindful walks in the woods, trying to expand my consciousness to include the woods around me. As I learned about these techniques, I realized that I have been taking mindful walks in the woods ever since I was a child. So this practice has always been part of my life. I just didn't have a name for it when I was young.

* * *

Carl Rogers and Abraham Maslow are the recognized founders of humanistic psychology, and both were interested in spiritual pursuits. Surprisingly, whereas Rogers came from a strong Christian background and actually trained to be a minister, Maslow was an atheist.

* * *

When Rogers was in college, during the early 1920s, he participated in a Christian fellowship program in which he traveled throughout the Far East. Rogers was fascinated by eastern philosophy and religion, and it eventually had a profound influence on his life and career. His work in psychology led him to focus on self-actualization, a much more positive approach to psychology and therapy than Freud's focus on the deep, dark unconscious mind.

Self-actualization refers to an individual having an innate tendency to be the best they can be. An important point is that this is *self*-actualization, our goals must be our own, as well as the benchmarks we use to judge our success. As we grow up, in order to develop a healthy personality we need to have others accept us for who we are, without preconceived expectations. In other words, we need to receive unconditional love from people who are important to us (such as our parents). That is the only way, according to Rogers, that we can continue to move toward achieving our ideal self while knowing that our real self is still somewhat inadequate. Of course, each time we achieve a major goal, and realize an aspect of our real self, then we adjust our ideal self by setting new and higher goals. For example, we might set the goal of finishing high school. When we do, we think about going to college. When we graduate from college, we might think about either a successful career or going on to graduate school. It is important to keep growing, to keep setting new goals, so that life is a continuous process of self-actualization.

* * *

Rogers began a major shift in perspective that many people in psychology have adopted toward psychotherapy. He believed that a therapist cannot "fix" their patient in the way that a medical doctor can fix a broken leg or give an antibiotic to kill some infection. So he began referring to the people he saw as "clients," and he developed the techniques we know today as client-centered therapy. In an article on the necessary and sufficient conditions for positive therapeutic change, Rogers listed six conditions which focus more on developing a healthy relationship between the therapist and client than they do on any other specific techniques. Simply put, it is an environment in which the client can experience the unconditional love they are lacking in their life. To me, this shift away from the medical model toward one which focuses on the person, not the disorder or problem, seems very compassionate. As I noted above, compassion is the ideal Buddhist emotional state. Thus, I view client-centered therapy as having been highly influence by Rogers' exposure to Buddhist philosophy.

* * *

Maslow made the study of self-actualization the focus of much of his career. Among other characteristics of self-actualized individuals, he described something he called a peak experience. A peak experience is a moment of awe and wonder, one loses sense of time and space, and it feels as if something extraordinary and transformative has occurred. However, Maslow also described these moments as "mystic experiences" or "oceanic feelings." The only difference between a peak experience and a mystic experience is whether or not the individual is spiritual, and willing to attribute such moments of lucidity to a deeper connection with God, or Tao, or some other essence of the universe. Indeed, as an atheist, Maslow believed that peak experiences were the explanation for past events in which prophets believed God had spoken to them. Could we actually know the difference?

I would say that it is possible to tell the difference between a peak experience and an actual mystic experience. I say this because I have had both, and the difference is extraordinary. Peak experiences are absolutely wonderful moments when it feels like everything in life has come together as the result of making good choices and putting in the effort to fulfill some goal. Mystic experiences, however, are quite different. They are unexpected, one might even say unexpectable. And when they occur, the feeling is more than just wonderful, indeed more than one can describe. They seem to arise from beyond any frame of reference available to us. This is where the term oceanic comes from. Like the ocean, it is simply too big to even imagine.

I give Maslow credit for coming up with a way to explain divine revelation, especially the sort of divine revelation that occurs when God speaks to one His prophets. For an atheist, this was necessary for Maslow. Yet I have to believe that he never had an oceanic or mystical experience. If he had, he might have understood the difference. Still, he suspected that there was something more. He proposed a 4th force in psychology (after psychodynamic theory, learning theory, and humanistic psychology). The 4th force was the domain of transcendent psychology, the sort of being needs that went beyond self-actualization. What lies beyond self-actualization? The answer is to transcend the self and focus on others, such as our family, friends, community, even the whole world. It is hard to imagine what Maslow might have done had he pursued this topic. Unfortunately, he died suddenly in his early 60s.

* * *

Although Rogers and Maslow were influenced by Buddhism and other eastern philosophies, there is a fundamental difference between humanistic psychology and Buddhism. Humanistic psychology focuses on self-actualization, whereas Buddhism teaches that there is no such thing as the self, it is merely an illusion. As contradictory as these theories may seem at first glance, Maslow actually laid a foundation for their compromise.

Maslow is perhaps best known for his hierarchy of needs. He believed that the lowest level needs must be satisfied first, before a person can attend to their higher needs. The first four levels, the so-called deficiency needs, are physiological, safety, belonging and love, and esteem needs. If we are deficient in any of these needs, we must satisfy them before we concern ourselves with higher needs. Standing above these deficiency needs is the one being need: self-actualization. So Maslow had qualitatively separated self-actualization from the needs associated with the bodily self (physiological and safety needs) and our immediate family, community, tribe, or whatever you want to call it (belongingness and esteem needs).

Buddhists believe in a single universal spirit. Our true self is that spark of spirit that exists within us, and that when we realize all of nature is temporary, that this body will die, we can then realize our true self. In other words, they do not associate the true self with a physical body. Even our thoughts are physical, since they arise from the function of neurons in the brain. As strange as it may first seem to Westerners to say that our body has nothing to do with whom we are, think about it. I recently lost over 30 pounds. Did I become less of a person? I am nearly 200 pounds heavier than when I was born. Was I only a fraction of a person when I was born? I have two artificial hip joints, made out of platinum and chromium. Am I not entirely human? You see, very clearly we are not our physical bodies. We are so much more!

* * *

Nonetheless, it would be foolish to ignore how closely we associate ourselves with our bodies, our possessions, our family and friends, all the 10 thousand things spoken of in the Tao Te Ching. I have cherished possessions, and letting go of my attachment to them is not something I look forward to. And yet, I have lost many precious things and life still goes on. So the Buddha taught us to let go of our attachments, and to accept life with equanimity. That is the path I am trying to following as I enter the second half of my life. Considering the nature of the first half of my life, I have lots of material upon which to focus my meditation.

Family – Grasping the First Half of Life

My family is not close. I'm not sure anybody really cares about anybody else. Maybe I have become too distant to see the relationships that do exist, but that distance is all that keeps me in contact. Otherwise, I think I would have severed ties with everyone long ago, rather than allow the ties to remain, and slowly, little by little, strengthen a bit, but only with certain people.

* * *

I'm pretty sure my father never wanted any children. He sure didn't seem to want anything to do with us after we grew up, or anything to do with his grandchildren. My parents were divorced when I was about 6 years old, and it was an ugly divorce. I have few memories of when we were still a family, and they generally aren't good. The great psychoanalyst Alfred Adler (one of my favorites) developed a psychological test based on early memories. He believed that if you examined a person's earliest key memories, it would tell you a lot about their personality. My earliest memory of my father is an interesting one.

When I was about 6 years old I was mauled by a neighbor's dog. I still have scars on my back, and I became terrified of all dogs. It was a typical example of a classically conditioned phobia. My parents didn't think it was good for a child to be so afraid of dogs, so they got me a dog. Thinking that a puppy might be too bouncy and nippy, they got me an adult dog, a dog as big as me, and I was terrified of it. But after a while, I came to love my dog. However, that did nothing to alter my phobia.

Rather than generalize my love for my dog to other dogs, I discriminated among them. I considered my dog to be a wonderful pet, but all other dogs were still vicious beasts hell-bent on killing me! Then my dog disappeared. My father told me he decided to give it away. I was devastated, but not nearly as bad as I was a few days later when my dog got hit by a car and killed. Since I blamed my dog's death on the new owner, for not taking care of him like I would have, I also blamed my father for killing my dog by giving him to that careless person.

Thirty years later I learned the truth. My dog had been killed by a car, and my parents didn't dare tell me. So my father lied to me about giving him away. Then, when I learned half of the truth, I made some erroneous conclusions. Remember, I was only about 6 years old. Nonetheless, this dramatically affected the nature of my relationship with my father for the rest of our lives. Of course, he never really did anything to change my impression of him. To my knowledge Adler never talked about more recent memories, but in my opinion, they have even more to say about my father.

* * *

When I was in my early 30s, my father and I were in his front yard in Arlington, Virginia. I was a research scientist with the National Institutes of Health. He was an administrator/scientist with the National Science Foundation. He said if there was one of his children he was really proud of, it was my brother Jeff. I was really pissed, but not surprised. I was used to not being good enough for him.

Around the same time, a guy down the street was selling his used car. My father said it was a great car, and I should think about buying it. I said I didn't have the money. He said too bad, I was missing out on a great car. A couple of years earlier my stepfather told my ex-wife and I that he had a friend selling a great used car. We said we didn't have the money to buy it. Gene bought the car and gave it to us. He said we could pay him when we had the money. And we did. Guess who was being a real father!

Shortly after my first son died, my in-laws, Gene and Elaine, came out to Maryland to visit and console us. I imagine they needed some consoling too, since Mark Jr. was their first grandchild. My father and his third wife came over one evening, and all night my father whined about how he had a bad cold, or the flu, or something. I really didn't give a damn. Unlike him, I wanted my children, and my first one had just died.

Finally, after Samuel was born, my father came to Samuel's first birthday party. He hardly spent any time there at all, and talked about himself the whole time (he had recently gotten his pilot's license). I was fed up. I have only talked to my father once or twice in some 14 years, and I have no interest in talking to him again. Thanks to some good psychotherapy, I am no longer angry. Now I just don't care about him. Turnabout is fair play.

* * *

By the way, as a psychologist I know that human memory is notoriously bad. But Adler recognized that early memories did not necessarily have to be correct. It was not the accuracy of the memory that mattered, but the underlying feelings that were conveyed. So if anyone wants to challenge anything I say in this book, feel free. Maybe my memories are mistaken, but I know how I feel. And those feelings are true.

The most important feeling I have from childhood goes right to the core of existential psychology. I felt that my life had no meaning. I am still plagued by these feelings today. I look at things I am doing, and I know, I really know, that I do some good things for many people. But I still can't

24

convince myself that my life has made a real difference. I always knew that my father considered me to be a disappointment. And my stepfather didn't help much.

* * *

Early on I had a good relationship with my stepfather. He loved sports, and I was a pretty good football player when I was in 6th-8th grade. One of his best friends was one of my football coaches. We both loved to fish, and I got to drive our boat out on the Atlantic Ocean. But at the same time, there were always problems. My brother never really seemed to get along with my stepfather, at least as far as I could tell, and he didn't have our father to turn to, so I always felt bad for my brother. And as the marriage between our mother and stepfather turned bad, really, really bad, things got ugly again.

When I was in high school, my bother left home, or at least was seldom around. It seems like my younger sister was seldom around (my father's 3rd child), and she eventually left home at a pretty young age. I was the only one around for a lot of the problems. I walked in on my stepfather screwing his best friend's wife on the living room couch. My mother attempted suicide a few times. My stepfather and I almost got into a fight once, but he backed down when I grabbed a dining room chair as a weapon.

When he finally left, I had a job working at the drugstore in town. My mom told me I had to pay room and board, since I had a regular job. I was 15 years old. But I didn't mind paying to live at home, because I knew my mom needed the money. I considered moving into my own place, figuring that if I was going to pay, I might as well make my own rules and come and go as I please. But I pretty much did that anyway, so it was still cheaper to stay.

* * *

Speaking of rules, one afternoon I called my mom an "asshole." She came storming into the room and yelled that I should watch what I say. I stood there and said I had, I had said exactly what I meant to say. So she threw her glass of vodka in my face. Then she called my father, and he came over a few days later.

My father told me that when he was young he had sworn at my grandmother. His father knocked him across the room for doing it. But my father said he wasn't going to hit me, because he was afraid I might hit him back. What a p*ssy! That's right, I said it. Rude, crude, and socially unacceptable, but that's how I felt, and no other word would capture the meaning in quite the same way. OK, I just went back and put in the asterisk,

25

so I didn't quite really say it or write it (thanks Danny and Chenika), but that's still how I felt at the time!

To this day I wonder if I would have hit my father. I want to know! But I never got the chance, because he didn't have the guts to do what he thought he should, and he didn't have the faith in me to take the chance. Some of you may think this is absolute foolishness, how can a professor of psychology advocate violence against a child? Well, the world used to be a different place. Not better, just different. And we all have our feelings about how we grew up, and what mattered in life. Being a man used to mean something. It may have meant something perverted, but if that's what it meant to you, then that is what it meant to you. My father told that he believed he should belt me for swearing at my mother, but he didn't do it. It was just another sad example of him not wanting to bother with his kids.

* * *

I thought that starting a family of my own would lead to a source of meaning in my life. I fell madly in love with Donna when I met her, and 25 years later I still love her just as much. I have 2 wonderful children, and still think fondly of the 9 months we had with our first son (who died at birth). My in-laws are great. Both Gene and Elaine, Donna's parents, have always been wonderful to me, and truly welcomed me into their family. I never had a lot in common with Donna's sister, but at various times I did a variety of things with both of her brothers, including rock climbing, softball, and fishing.

When we were first married, and Donna was in school and I was a postdoctoral research fellow, we enjoyed many a free meal with her parents. I must point out that they were very good meals too; I loved their cooking, especially when Gene was grilling. Gene and I also shared an interest in both fine wine and good, economical wine. We would often share our latest find in terms of a quality wine at a good price.

Now that Donna has left me, I almost never see anyone in her family. For 25 years they have been a very, very important part of my life. But now it seems strange, as if I am no longer related to them. Once in a while I see Gene and Elaine at one of our children's activities, but I don't see anyone else. I miss them, especially my Godson Ben. Friends have told me I have every right to see them, but that isn't the point. I can't bear the pain of seeing them, knowing that their daughter/sister/aunt dumped me. How do I talk about that? How can I not, and still be true to my own feelings? I sure as hell can't stand the thought of visiting the in-laws and then having Donna show up with a new boyfriend.

* * *

26

I mentioned that I have two wonderful children, but Donna and I had three children. I often shock my psychology students by telling them that the best news I ever got in my life was my first child's autopsy. Mark David Kelland, Jr. died as the result of a birth defect called an omphalocele. It occurs in about 1/5,000 births, and can often be treated with surgery. However, our son's autopsy showed that he had additional, severe complications. He did not develop lungs, and could not have survived after birth. It was this information, the knowledge that there was absolutely nothing they could have done to save our son, that was such good news (under the circumstances). I can't imagine how much more devastated I would have felt if the autopsy had revealed that our son had a chance if only the doctors had known about the omphalocele in advance. I really can't imagine feeling more devastated than I did when I lost my first child.

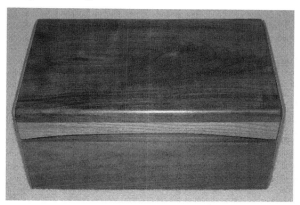

The cedar chest containing mementos of Mark Kelland, Jr. His grandfather Gene Zawisa made the chest by hand.

When I think about accepting my life as it is, and letting go of my family as the first half of my life comes to an end, I find it very difficult to say farewell to Mark Jr., even though it has been 18 years. When a child dies, the parents become members of a secret group of caring people. Many people have lost a child, but never talk about it. When someone they know even only barely, such as other people who work in the same building, loses a child, they offer their condolences through shared grief. They tell you about their child, and you know they truly share your pain. You know they *understand* how bad it hurts! Then, after a week or two, the deaths are once again not spoken of, until the next child dies. I have mentioned this to a fair number of people, and they have all agreed that this phenomenon is real. I consider it to be one of the most fascinating aspects of the human community I have ever experienced.

* * *

So, in terms of the Vedic stages of life, I have an interesting background. During the first stage of life, I belonged to an uncaring family. One where I never felt that I fit in, where I was never appreciated, where all my efforts to get others to care about something, anything, were for naught. During the second stage of life, I found a wonderful new family, people who welcomed me, cared for me, made me feel loved, and whom I cared for just as much. Yet now they are essentially gone as well.

I am now supposedly ready to begin the third stage of life, or as Jung would describe it, the second half of life, the cultural period. The challenge for me is that all I am doing in terms of cultural development, or in line with the Vedic stage of forest-dweller (my spiritual development), was neither a simple nor a comfortable transition. My wife of 23 years shattered my existence; she destroyed nearly every aspect of my householder life, leaving me adrift. I simply did not have the opportunity to shift my focus from my family to my contributions to the community, I was thrust into it an abyss against my will. Now what!?

The German existentialist Martin Heidegger used a term which has new meaning for me: being-thrown-into-this-world. It describes how we are in conflict with the reality of this mysterious world and our desire to control it. Unfortunately, it is absolutely impossible to control the world, since we eventually realize that we are going to die! We then experience a great deal of anxiety. Only accepting death can lead to the desire to fully experience life, to achieve a sense of being-in-the-world. I needed a little more time. I am just starting to learn this stuff, just starting to follow this path. I thought I would have family with me to help, in part through helping them, or at least just being with them, perhaps sitting on the deck, sipping a glass of wine, waiting for the food on the grill to be done. But life doesn't worry about accommodating our schedules.

Family – Abandoning the Second Half of Life?

Why put a question mark at the end of this chapter's title? For one thing, I might be dead tomorrow. I don't expect that will happen, but we never really know. I'm also not sure what "abandoning" means. What I am trying to refer to is the goal of being unattached to the future, having no expectations of where my life will lead me and what, if any, role my family may play in that future. How that will affect my current relationships, only time will tell. But having arrived at a place I never imagined, I don't intend to have a plan from this point forward. Having such a plan can only lead to disappointment, because life follows its own path.

Nonetheless, I do wonder about the future, and I toy with different possibilities. Despite a desire to achieve true non-attachment, let's begin with the two relationships I really care about: my children Samuel and John. I believe I have helped them to understand that they must take care of themselves, that although I hope to always be there for them, what I have to offer is limited. Whatever I have I will freely give it to them if they ask, but I hope they don't come asking for money too often! Perhaps this is why I have tried to teach them that some things are worth more than money, and one's goals in life should be more spiritual than financial.

* * *

Samuel seems to be on a good path. The reason I say that is that he is not on a path that I ever expected for him. He loves music, and is considering majoring in music in college. He definitely did not get that from me. I love listening to a wide variety of music, from Krishna Das to Black Sabbath, but when it comes to playing an instrument I am hopeless. Samuel currently plays five instruments (tuba, sousaphone, guitar [acoustic and electric], bass guitar, and harmonica). He plays in the orchestra, marching band, jazz band, the district honor's band, and at home he and his friends typically play rock and heavy metal. We do

29

share a favorite band right now, *The Used*.

Last month *The Used* played at the Orbit Room in Grand Rapids, MI. I got tickets for us to go, and Samuel bought some cards that gave us a chance to meet the band after the show and get autographs. As we were getting our autographs I mentioned to the lead singer, Bert McCracken, that I really liked *Lies for Liars*. I first heard it when my ex-wife was planning to divorce me, and there had been plenty of lies along the way. I had to whisper it to him, because I didn't want Samuel to hear exactly what I said. Bert laughed, and stuck out his fist for a fist bump. Samuel had a funny look on his face, which I interpreted as "Wow, dad's pretty cool!" I have no idea whether or not that's what Samuel actually thought, but that's the memory I'm going with, because I want to. It was a good night, especially since Samuel and I don't have much else in common.

* * *

As for my younger son, John, we have lots in common. We like to fish, hunt, watch sports, and we have similar nasty tempers. We have had some fights over the years, but we both also get over it pretty quick. What is really amusing, after the fact, is that when I try to remain mindful and calm, and encourage him to do the same, he just mocks me. He knows that deep down inside I have a temper like his, and he doesn't believe I can control it forever. But we both seem to be trying, and things have gotten a lot better.

I also don't want to suggest that we fight all the time. We have some pretty good days together, especially when he gets the better of me on a fishing trip. John also runs track, and I was a pretty good runner before I was disabled. But even more interestingly, John is considering a career in chemical engineering. Since much of the research I did when I was younger involved experimental pharmacology, I still have something of an interest in biochemistry. Although only in 8th grade, John is beginning to think about college, which suggests that he will focus well on his studies in high school. Whatever direction he ends up following, he will have my full support. Just as I have learned to not worry about where my life may be going, I am not worried about the direction of my children's lives. They seem to be doing just fine.

* * *

There are many other people in my family, and it is quite interesting to consider the nature of being unattached to them. First, there is an individual: my ex-wife. Second, there is my ex-wife's family. And finally, there is my own family. I will consider each in turn.

What of my ex-wife? For 25 years she was my best friend. We had three children together, and one of them died. We finished graduate school together, began our careers together, and co-authored a research article and a textbook supplement. We moved from Michigan to Maryland (first son), back to Michigan (second son), then to New Hampshire (third son), and finally back to Michigan again (where I was a stay-at-home dad for a year). We went to a lot of marriage counseling, and then she started dating. Then she divorced me, and it was all over, except for the kids, the dogs, the upside-down mortgage on the house we couldn't sell if we wanted to, and the looming cost of college. So it's kind of difficult to be completely unattached, at least in terms of material things.

But here's the real problem: I love her. I love her as much as the day I met her. And *nothing* will ever change that. I doubt I could ever stand to be with her again, and it really bothers me that our children are not happy about the situation, but still I love her. It makes me wonder whether love is a good thing or a bad thing. Love seems to be the primary source of my emotional pain. I understand that non-attachment is not about putting an end to caring about other people. The ideal Buddhist emotional state is one of compassion, and I truly regret that my ex-wife feels as if she has wasted so much of her life. I'm not just guessing here, she basically said that once, though she used different words. What she actually said was that she had spent 20 years with her parents, and then 20 years with me. What was her life going to be like in another 20 years? Ouch!

Let me say that again: Ouch!

I love my in-laws. I have always gotten along great with my father-in-law, and almost always gotten along great with my mother-in-law (the only iffy times are actually a little amusing in retrospect). At different times I was friends with each brother-in-law, and I have enjoyed some healthy debates with my sister-in-law. So I don't think my ex-wife should paint such a bleak picture of her family life. Or such a bleak picture of our life together.

Nonetheless, she feels that she has missed out on something. But I wonder if she even knows what that something is. What will her life be like in 20 years? If you don't know what you're looking for, it may be impossible to find it. I hope and I pray that she does, but I realize that I won't be there to help her. Granted, I also won't be there to get in the way. But when you love someone, it is hard to just let go.

* * *

As for my own family, as noted above, we have never been close. So the relationship I have is a good example of being unattached. I care about my mother, my brother, and my sisters, but our relationships are both physically and emotionally distant. This allows casual contact on an intermittent basis, but occasionally I reach out a little bit more. And the consequences have been very interesting. I would like to share two particular visits.

When my brother's daughter graduated from college, no one bothered to invite me to the party. They figured I wouldn't drive from Michigan to Massachusetts. However, as a college professor, I like to encourage education. So when my mom mentioned the party and found out I wasn't invited, she told my sister to invite me. When I got the invitation I called my mom and told her I was coming. But, I told her to keep it a secret from everyone else. When we walked in, my niece threw her arms around me and yelled "Uncle Mark, you came!" My brother was pretty amazed, and everybody was completely surprised. We had a good time that evening.

The last time I visited, however, was not so much fun. At a family dinner, everyone started ripping on me for being a lousy professor. Now, none of them has ever been in my classroom, or met any of my students, or read any of my student evaluations, but they had read a few reviews on RateMyProfessor.com. I have an interesting teaching style, which most students like, but some don't. I have 32 ratings on this website, out of the thousands of students I have taught over the years. Overall they are pretty good, but a few people didn't like my class. This was the basis for my brother and sister coming to the conclusion that I am no good at my career. Suffice it to say, I was pissed.

After everyone left, I got into an argument with my mother. When I complained about how I had been treated, she said that's just how family treats each other. "No it isn't," I said. I didn't drive 800 miles to insult and degrade people, and the people insulting and degrading me were wrong. And even if there were any truth to what they were saying, they should have been more considerate of the fact that I was in the middle of a divorce and very depressed. They could have been nice. My mother said I shouldn't take it personally. How the hell do you not take that personally? After a while of pointless arguing, I finally said that maybe I just wouldn't ever visit again. She got upset, and thought I was overacting. But I simply said again that if I was

32

going to be put down when I visited, I wouldn't bother to visit. They would have to be the ones to live with that.

* * *

I haven't been to Massachusetts since that night, but I didn't have any other reason to be. This summer I was hoping to go to Maine, but I don't have a lot of money due to my divorce. I really don't know how I feel right now, but I do know that I don't feel any need to visit family.

Sometimes people say stupid things. Family is forever. Blood is thicker than water. I believe the only people who matter in your life are the ones who care about you. And I don't mean the ones who say they care, or pretend they care; I mean the ones who actually care. They might be family or they might not be. But my advice is simple: when people mistreat you, let go. Let go completely, don't carry any baggage around with you. That's the only way to be free. If they hold it against you, try to feel compassion for how trapped they are by their own negativity. But don't get drawn back into dysfunctional relationships.

* * *

So I have two children I love and truly care about. I look forward to the day when they have families of their own. I like the idea of having grandchildren, when the time is right. I wonder if I will live long enough to have great-grandchildren. That would be cool. But there are no expectations.

I pray that my children will find happiness, but I know how elusive that can be. I hope they develop a sense of personal integrity, something that provides meaning in their lives, some purpose as they march forward through this thing we call life.

I wonder if I will ever be in an intimate relationship again. I get lonely, but I embrace my aloneness. I enjoy solitude, especially when hiking mindfully through the woods. Of course, those quiet moments are often the times you really want to share with someone you love: a glancing look, a little smile, just knowing that someone is with you and sharing that precious moment of contentment. Yeah, I miss that, and I get lonely. When I move back home I should have my dog again. Sunny is cool; and we get along really well. Having a dog or a cat may not be a substitute for a girlfriend or boyfriend, but pets seldom betray you, and their love is truly unconditional.

But what will life be like when I get really old? Will I be visiting with my children and their wives and my grandchildren? Or might they move away, making visits difficult? Will I be back in my house, or maybe have moved on from there? Will I even live that long? There is simply no way to tell. But I do know that I will have a little altar for meditation wherever I live. Meditation helps to keep me focused and mindful. I should do it more.

* * *

A couple of days after I thought this chapter might be done, something happened which I thought would be interesting to share. My ex-wife had just returned from a weekend getaway with her new lover. I spent as much time with my kids as they could bear, both being teenagers who have more important things to do than hang around with dad (which for them is just about anything else). After my ex-wife came home, she sent me an email to remind me she was having a minor surgery in a few days. Not being too happy about where she had been for the weekend, I sent a simple reply saying that I remembered, and if she needed any help, just let me know.

Because my reply was so short, she thought I was being inconsiderate and cold-hearted. She sent a message to a friend, who I am also sort of friends with from before our divorce. Her friend sent an interesting reply, which she accidentally sent to me, instead of to my ex-wife. Thinking the email was about my ex-wife's weekend with her lover, and confused by the odd wording of the email which talked about fire and ice in relationships, I became very upset with my ex-wife. I focused on the fire part, and thought she had been talking to her friend about the passion in her new relationship. But actually, the focus of the email was on the ice, and that was a reference to me and to how cold-hearted I seemed to them because of my short message.

When things got cleared up, I sent the following email to my ex-wife's friend. It demonstrates how fragile my psyche is still:

Dear ...,

It hurts me even more to learn that the email was about me. I can't believe that either of you think I am so cold-hearted. Try to see things from my point of view.

I gave Donna my whole heart, without reservations. As many times as I may have failed to satisfy her, everything I did was for us and for our children. I was faithful to the weddings vows I took, and I remain so today. It was my own foolishness for giving my heart completely to a woman who never really loved me, and it is my own curse that now there is no taking it back. I am terribly lonely, and still find it hard to believe that she has left me behind and so quickly found a new love.

This past weekend, Donna got to enjoy a nice getaway. During my spring break she was on vacation in Florida. She has another long weekend getaway coming up in about a month. Saturday night John asked me if I could get a movie. I had to ask him to pay for it himself. Can you even begin to imagine how humiliating it is to have to tell my children that I don't even have $5 dollars for a movie, while their mom can afford vacations and weekend getaways? Do you have any clue how searingly painful it is to sit at home alone on a pleasant evening, knowing that the woman you love and her lover are enjoying the nice house and the nice deck that you helped build for a family that just walked away from you, because you weren't good enough to satisfy that woman you love so deeply?

I helped Donna through graduate school. I helped her establish her career. I helped her raise our children. Even she admits I was at my best when our first son died. I did not hesitate to return to Michigan for her career. Even now I still set up her online courses at LCC so she can make some extra money. And what do I have to show for it? Nothing! I struggle to get by from paycheck to paycheck, because I give her so much money that both the mediator and Donna's lawyer asked me how I expected to pay my bills with what was left. But I swore that I would never fight her over the settlement, because I would never do anything that would drag the children into the middle of our problems.

But none of this was the reason my email was so short. It was not short because I am heartless. It was short because I am heartbroken. I realized that if Donna really did need something or someone, she would likely call the man she loves. And that is NOT me!

I am barely hanging on by a thread. I struggle desperately to find any source of meaning in my life. My best friend for 25 years disappeared when Donna left me, and I never did anything to hurt that friendship (as something separate from our marriage). Please try to understand that my life has ended, and I cannot see an alternative life. I don't want to see an alternative life, though I know the past is over.

I will be praying for Donna to come through her surgery well. I have told her how much I will always love her. But if Donna has any questions about whether or not I am cold-hearted, she only has to look within herself. Because she has my heart.

I will copy this email to Donna, so you need have no concerns about whether or not to share any of this with her. Thank you for having been such a good friend for Donna. It comforts me to know that she has such a true and caring friend.

With deepest humility,
Mark

My Career

For many men, their career defines who they are. I suppose the same is true for a small number of women as well. This social phenomenon once served an important purpose. If only one person in a village knew an important trade skill, such as being a blacksmith, someone else had to learn the trade in order for the skills to be passed on. It was only natural for that man's son(s) to work by the father's side, learning the trade. Similarly, the children of farming families typically stayed on the farm, raised their families there, and continued farming the land. The world today, however, is quite different. More and more people go to college and pursue a career that may have nothing to do with the paths followed by their parents.

A more serious problem with this tradition is the economy today. As companies downsize (I will not call it right-sizing), or go bankrupt, people who have devoted their entire careers to that company are tossed aside like any other disposable resource. Now I know this is a complex issue, and there are multiple perspectives on these processes, but the point is that if you have invested your identity in such a company, what then? Does the loss of your position lead to the loss of self-esteem, self-respect, even self-identity? Again, this depends entirely on the individual.

* * *

In high school I took a vocational aptitude test. The results suggested that I should be a psychologist, a biologist, or a mortician. I know I had depression and anger issues when I was young, but is that what suggested I should work with dead bodies? It seems to me that morticians need a lot of people skills, and I didn't think of myself as being good at that. Strange then, that I thought psychology was a good choice. I loved my psychology class in high school, but that was partly because I had a great teacher and partly because it was research that fascinated me, as opposed to therapy. I also really enjoyed my biology classes, but none of this really affected my choice of which college to attend. The only factor that influenced that decision was William J. O'Reilly.

Bill O'Reilly was an important father-figure in my life. I mowed his lawn, shoveled the snow from his driveway, and eventually worked in the Rexall drugstore owned by Mr. and Mrs. O'Reilly. They were both pharmacists, so was their eldest daughter, and they had all attended the Massachusetts College of Pharmacy. So I decided to attend that college as well. I did OK my first year, but during the summer I enlisted in the U. S. Marine Corps Reserve and had a good ole time at Parris Island, South Carolina. I returned to school in the fall, and began my reserve duty of one weekend a month. I also began a new job as a security guard at a hospital in Boston, where the Massachusetts College of Pharmacy is located. It was also the year I began drinking alcohol in earnest.

I steadily drank more and more. Eventually I dropped out of college, got in trouble at work, my girlfriend dumped me, and I got in some serious trouble with the law. I'm sure the statute of limitations on the stuff we did has long since passed, but I will avoid going into detail because I am simply ashamed of some of the stuff we did, not that anything was truly terrible (at least we didn't kill anybody; there is no statute of limitations on murder). However, I will say that the time came when the police wanted to talk with me. A detective from District 2 in Boston called me one morning, and asked if he could arrest me over the phone. I said I had a few errands to take care of, and I would stop by the police station that afternoon. That's just what I did, and when I got there I told him everything he needed to know, including the fact that I was simply guilty. From that point forward, the detective was on my side. Later, he spoke on my behalf to the judge, telling him that I had cooperated, and that I really wanted to overcome my alcoholism and make amends for what I had done wrong. The judge agreed to continue the case without finding, I paid some restitution, showed up six months later having been sober for six months, and a finding of *not guilty* was entered. So what does this have to do with my career?

When I realized I needed to get back to school, I was embarrassed to go back to the school I had dropped out of, so I transferred to Northeastern University. I went to night school so I could work, and I switched my major to psychology. I did very well at Northeastern, made the Dean's list, and applied for graduate school. One of my professors looked at the schools I was applying to, and suggested that I might get in, but that I might not get full funding for graduate school, because I didn't have the best experience (such as having done some research while an undergrad, and I had all those Fs from the Massachusetts College of Pharmacy on my transcript). So I considered some other schools that were very good, but not as well known and perhaps not as competitive. One of those schools was Wayne State University, and off I went to Michigan. I earned my Ph.D. in physiological psychology as Wayne State was embarking on a dramatic expansion, helping to transform part of the city of Detroit. I am very proud to have attended an excellent, inner-city college, and it eventually had an unexpected influence on the direction of my career.

* * *

My advisor in graduate school, David Asdourian, didn't have a particularly impressive research career, but he did a couple of things that really worked to my advantage. He had been on sabbatical the year I applied, so he was returning to campus as I was arriving on campus. He had some interesting new ideas, but wasn't really sure how to implement them. After some hasty training, he pretty much turned me loose. Since I tend to be the kind of person who gets things done, it was an ideal opportunity for me. The research for my master's thesis was done in less than two years, and that project led directly into my dissertation research. Both papers were published, and I was done with my Ph.D. in less than four years.

I was also introduced to Lou Chiodo, who had worked in Wayne State's physiological psychology labs as an undergraduate. Dr. Chiodo had recently returned to Michigan to join a new research institute at Sinai Hospital in Detroit, and I had the opportunity to work in his laboratory while I was still in graduate school. I continued on as a postdoctoral research fellow.

Lou came from a high-pressure/high-stakes background, having attended graduate school at Yale University studying under a very well-known research psychiatrist. Since this was a new laboratory, and Lou was attempting to solidify his place in the field of dopamine electrophysiology, I was again provided with some quick training and then supported in everything I wanted to do. Before long, I was publishing steadily, reviewing papers for journals, and getting to know the right people in my field.

I moved on to the National Institute of Neurological Disorders and Stroke, working with Judy Walters. I continued working on some interesting projects, challenging some accepted beliefs in our field of research. I collaborated with the adjacent behavioral neuroscience group, became a founding member of the International Behavioral Neuroscience Society, served on the Animal Care and Use Committee, and had some opportunities to review grants. Of particular interest was the work I collaborated on with Bob Boldry, who worked in the laboratory of Tom Chase. We worked on a project that seemed to refute a new line of research coming out of the laboratory of Arvid Carlsson, who soon thereafter shared the Nobel Prize in Medicine for classic research done years earlier. Our results were confirmed, but we were actually rather disappointed. It had seemed that Dr. Carlsson was identifying a new treatment for Parkinson's disease, with a class of relatively safe drugs. Unfortunately, it ultimately turned out that the animal model being used wasn't really appropriate for the new class of drugs. Still, to think that I was correctly refuting research done in the laboratory of an eventual Nobel Laureate was a serious boost to my ego! Little did I suspect that a long-term research career was *not* in my future.

* * *

After working with Judy Walters for a couple of years, I rejoined Lou Chiodo's lab, which was now in the neuroscience program at the Wayne State University Medical School. I continued an interesting line of research I had begun in his lab a few years earlier and continued with Judy Walters. I outlined a number of interesting phenomena pertaining to the influences of different types of anesthesia on midbrain electrophysiological studies of the dopamine systems. I was able to replicate a variety of results that were being obtained by different laboratories using different techniques. Further, I was able to address why their results were different, which was based in large part on differences in the surgical use of anesthesia.

I also submitted my first major, successful grant, in which I proposed to study an intriguing new model of schizophrenia. In addition to studying the model at the cellular level, I was going to expand my research to include behavioral research. A major problem arose, however, in that Lou Chiodo decided to leave Wayne State for a position at Texas Tech University. At the time, the psychiatry department at Wayne State was in the middle of looking for a new department chair. So I didn't have anyone to talk to about my future in Detroit. Thus, I went on the job market as well. I eventually joined the psychology department at St. Anselm College in New Hampshire, and I arrived with the largest research grant in the school's history. Little by little, however, my career began to change direction.

* * *

At St. Anselm College I was often reminded that teaching was more important than research. I had no problem with that point of view, because I have always loved to teach. However, most of what we teach in psychology is based on research, so to suggest that my research was somehow a problem for my teaching was, in my opinion, a misguided perspective. Nonetheless, being a practical person, I used my research grant to benefit students at the college as much as I could. I hired a couple of students as part-time lab techs, and eventually hired one of them full-time after he graduated. When we went to local conferences I would get a hotel room for one of the young men who worked in my lab, and another for one of the young women who worked in my lab, and then a whole bunch of students would pile into both rooms for free. When the dean suggested that they might bend the rules about offering release time from teaching for research, since I was doing so much for the college, I declined to even be considered for it. I enjoyed my teaching, and had students doing more and more of the research.

At the same time, I was becoming interested and active in the field of service-learning. I started attending conferences held by the New Hampshire College and University Council, then implemented two new programs, and finally began presenting at NHCUC conferences. This led to a small grant to host a service-learning workshop at St. A's, and then an invitation to write a chapter for a national monograph on service-learning.

So now I had both an active biomedical research program and an active service-learning program. The eventual highlight came after three years, at one of the graduation ceremonies. Each year St. A's presented two senior thesis awards to a graduating senior. This was a great honor for the students, and an intense competition amongst the faculty. Having one of your students chosen for this award was basically equivalent to winning an award for faculty member of the year. One of my students, Megan Kazlauskas won one of these awards, for research on the Stargazer mutant rat. These rats are a model for Tourette Syndrome, and they respond well to antipsychotic medication (as do patients with Tourette Syndrome). Megan demonstrated that these rats do not demonstrate deficits associated with schizophrenia in an animal model of that disorder (thus helping to confirm the specificity of the Stargazer rat as a model of Tourette Syndrome).

At the same time, I used that animal model of schizophrenia to demonstrate, for the first time, that nicotine functions as an antipsychotic medication. For years schizophrenic patients had been telling their doctors that nicotine reduced their symptoms, and I finally put it to the test in an appropriate animal model (a model which had been validated with humans). An influential neuroscientist took an interest in the poster I presented that year in Cancun at the International Behavioral Neuroscience Society meeting, and offered to connect me with some research folks at a tobacco company. I was on the verge of becoming a tobacco industry whore! I often wonder how much research money I could have gotten for publishing research on how cigarettes help people who are psychotic. But my days of research were numbered, and that was one of the last major scientific conferences I attended.

* * *

My wife had been offered a job back in Michigan, where she was born and raised. I liked Michigan, and I wanted our children to grow up near their mom's family, so we headed back to Michigan. I spent a year commuting back and forth between Michigan and New Hampshire, and spent nearly a year as a stay at home dad. I was eventually offered two jobs. Alice Young, a professor of psychology at Wayne State had become an associate dean, and was looking for someone to run her laboratory. I have always regretted that I didn't work with her when I was in graduate school, and it seemed like a wonderful opportunity. However, she didn't want me to teach, and it was a soft-money position with little security (indeed, a few years later, she left Wayne St.).

I had also been offered a position at Lansing Community College, where I would certainly get to teach, but my research career would come to an end. On the plus side, it was a tenure-track position, with no pressure to

41

publish or get grants. As I said above, I love to teach, and I was getting more and more involved in educational programs at St. A's, so the opportunity for tenure was suddenly far more attractive than conducting research.

* * *

I have now been teaching at Lansing Community College for 13 years. It's a really easy position. You just teach your classes from the end of August to the beginning of May, and then take 3 months vacation. You don't have to write grants, and you don't have to publish anything. It really is a breeze.

Funny thing, though, it seems the people who only do that bare minimum are among the ones who whine the most about how hard they have to work. What a joke! I have done anything but the bare minimum, and in this economy I am very happy to have a job. I don't mind working for my pay. In fact, I consider it a moral imperative, considering how badly some people are struggling today.

So what have I been doing to take the place of the inherent drive that used to push me to excel in my research career? I helped to establish a new service-learning program here at LCC. I became active in our virtual college, and served as a liaison and mentor for our department and some of our faculty. I wrote a supplemental textbook, an article on service-learning, a personality textbook, and then both an article and a book on Buddhist mindfulness and martial arts programs for people with physical disabilities based on my first sabbatical leave. I have earned three different black belts, I am studying two new martial arts, and I started my own business to teach martial arts to people with physical disabilities. I have developed new courses, and taught an honor's course. And all of this had been done while I am usually teaching an overload, often because the college needs me, but the extra money comes in quite handy since my divorce.

* * *

A few days ago I met someone at the park who asked me what I was doing with my computer there. I love to write in the Highland Recreation Area, on a hill overlooking Teeple Lake. It is a beautiful spot, and sometimes I will put my computer away and go fishing. Teeple Lake has some very nice largemouth bass. Other

times I grab my camera and take advantage of photo opportunities, such as this picture of a great blue heron. I told her I was writing my third book, so she asked me if I was a writer. I said no, but maybe I ought to be, or maybe I am, but really I just find myself writing more and more.

Half way through my textbook, I vowed I would never write another book. Then I got the idea for this book. But this book was put on hold, as I began writing the book about my sabbatical leave. I also have an idea for a children's book, and a colleague at work recently gave a talk on self-publishing. She wrote a book for her daughter. So maybe I will get started on that fourth book after this one. But children's books are hard. They are short, so they must really capture the imagination without saying much. And you need a good illustrator; at least I do, because my artistic drawing abilities are limited to say the least.

As for another textbook, there is no way. It was far too much work, and I did it only because I had what I believed was a really good approach at the right time (and my editor agreed). I have not had so much as an inkling of another idea for a textbook; the ones I am using are just fine. In fact, there are too many good ones, making it hard to choose for new faculty.

Physical Fitness and Physical Disability

I was always a pretty good athlete. Not great, but pretty good. I played football, owned a horse, played volleyball at the YMCA, became a long-distance runner, then started rock climbing, ice climbing, and alpine climbing, and finally got seriously into martial arts. I used to ride my bicycle 200-300 miles a week, both for exercise and just getting around to where my horse was stabled and then to work. To some extent, sports have always been part of my life.

This is not to say that age, children, and a busy career didn't take their tolls. Through my 30s and 40s I slowly gained weight and lost the edge on my conditioning. I would fight back from time to time, but other priorities would take over again and I would lose ground. I was clearly overweight, but not obese. It seemed as if my wife though differently. I was constantly being put down. What made this particularly difficult for me was that when she had gotten a little overweight I still loved her for who she was. Clearly, she was more interested in a vision of who she was married to than the man she had actually married. Indeed, the first affair I knew about was with a guy she met at the gym. I believe she also met the guy she is dating now at the gym. As much as this hurt to begin with, it set a very dangerous stage for what was happening with my physical condition.

When I began Taekwondo, I suffered several predictable injuries. I say they were predictable because of my age, my condition, and how competitive I am. As I listened to the wisdom of my own body, and backed away from pushing so hard, everything began to heal. At least, almost everything was healing. My hips just kept getting worse. I knew things were bad when the chiropractor I had started seeing said I really needed to get to an orthopedic surgeon. Somehow, this told me two things. One, she must be a good, professional chiropractor. I must admit that before seeing her I was one of the people who are very suspicious about the whole field of chiropractic. Two, if my chiropractor was saying she couldn't help me with my hips, I must really have needed to see an orthopedic surgeon.

* * *

I was a little nervous about seeing the orthopedic surgeon, but more than that, I felt like I was being a baby. I knew how much my hips hurt, and on some days I almost could not walk, but still I felt like I should be able to work my way through it. Then I sat down with my surgeon to look at my x-rays. Between both hip sockets there was only one little spot of cartilage left, and there was a bone spur there. And the arthritis was at level 3.5 out of 4.0. Now keep in mind, I was still practicing Taekwondo in this condition! I was

45

anything but a baby, my surgeon was pretty surprised that I was still doing some of the things I was doing. Nonetheless, it was bad news overall, because I was *not* going to get better.

We tried some physical therapy and hyaluronic acid injections first. It was a pretty interesting experience having hyaluronic acid injected directly into my hips sockets. The first injection was bearable, but the second injection was intensely painful. Afterward, the doctor who did the injection (my surgeon's partner) told me that the second injection was often very painful. I suggested that he might have told me that to begin with, and I don't really remember what he said about that. Maybe I was still in too much pain to remember.

An X-ray of the implant in the author's left hip.

These treatments helped a little bit, but only for a while. Hyaluronic acid helps cartilage to grow, but I didn't have any cartilage left. So we finally made the decision to go ahead with hip replacement surgery. I delayed the surgery for a while, in order to earn my black belt in Taekwondo. I had been told that I probably wouldn't be able to do martial arts after the surgery, and I had always wanted a black belt. So one month after getting my black belt, I went under the knife. The surgery went well, but recovery was hampered by the fact that I still needed another hip replacement. That came six months later, but not without a little drama in between.

* * *

During the medical screening for my first surgery, they noticed an abnormality in my EKG. This was a little surprising, because I'd had a cardiac stress test several years earlier when I first began taking high blood pressure medication. There is a long history of high blood pressure, heart attack, and stroke in my family. They said the abnormality wasn't too bad, and I could have another cardiac stress test when I was able to get on the treadmill after my first hip replacement. When that finally occurred, things got even more interesting. I will never forget reading that annoying letter which said I was fine, except for the thing that was not fine, and I needed to make an appointment for a more advanced cardiac test with Doppler radar! OK, maybe it isn't Doppler radar, but it is a Doppler measurement of blood flow, and don't ask me to explain it in any more detail than that.

So imagine what I was thinking. I am recovering from one major surgery, waiting for another. Then the letter says my heart is fine, except for the thing that isn't fine, and I need more advanced testing because they aren't even sure how bad the other thing might be. It is not an oversight on my part that I have not named what they were concerned about. The letter did not say. So I had no idea! I tried to convince myself it must not be too bad, or they would have called on the phone and had me come in immediately. Nonetheless, I was sure I was going to need open-heart surgery, and would have to delay my second hip replacement, and God only knows what else was going on inside my chest! When I complained about the letter to my personal doctor, she didn't seem to think I should have reacted the way I did, but said she would talk to her colleagues about changing the letter a little bit.

The concern was that I might have a prolapsed valve, which allows blood to flow back into the heart in the wrong direction after a beat. It is that blood flow that the doppler test specializes in observing. The test turned out normal, and they said I was OK and could go ahead with my hip replacement surgery. Then the technician asked me when I'd had my heart attack!

I never knew I had a heart attack, but she said that's what everything looked like. I have heard of silent heart attacks, and now I wonder if indeed I've had one. Then one day I had an interesting thought, maybe I had my heart attack when I left my body and went to heaven. Maybe I was so far removed from my body during that brief trip to heaven that it left behind some measurable effect in my EKG.

* * *

The candle burns soft,
Souls awaken with each breath,
God is silent with us.

If you skipped over the Preface, this is the same poem. I think it's a nice poem, which really surprises me. I am not the poetic type. Don't ask me exactly what the poetic type is, but I'm sure I am not one of them. There was something special about the retreat where I wrote this poem, and the highlight was my visit to heaven.

It was a five day silent retreat, with five hours of meditation a day. During our free time, I typically continued my meditation by mindfully walking through the gardens. Near the end of the retreat, during a meditation

47

before dinner, we were all in the meditation hall preparing ourselves. I believe it was the day after I wrote the poem. I entered into a very deep and peaceful meditation, and soon became aware of the feeling that I was rising out of my body. As I dared to look up, but only with the vision of my spirit as opposed to opening my physical eyes, I beheld a beautiful sight. I was in heaven.

In *Paradisio*, Dante describes a very similar experience. In the distance there is a beautiful light, and all around you that light glows with a perfect beauty that defies description. But what cannot be described at all, is the feeling of being immersed in perfect love and compassion. It felt perfect; more wonderful by far than anything I have ever experienced here on earth. I was overwhelmed by a strange feeling which combined being thrilled with being very simply content. I knew that I was in heaven, I really knew. In the distance, as if it were only a dream, I heard the gong signal the end of meditation. But I chose to stay in heaven. In the distance, I heard people leaving the meditation hall. Still, I chose to stay in heaven, forever!

But as I was being bathed in this perfect love and contentment, I heard a voice whisper in my ear. For a long time I assumed it was an angel, but now I wonder if it was my first son. The voice said very simply, "If you don't go back now, you will never see your wife and children again." Curiously, I was not told I had to go back. I was given a choice, free will. I realized I would particularly miss helping my children grow up, and that was all it took. I dropped back into my body and I was back in the real world.

It was suddenly a horrible feeling. I had left heaven! I wanted to go back to heaven, but it was too late. Very quickly I appreciated the blessing I had received, and knew that my place was still here in this world, with my children and my wife (though she later chose otherwise). I was still a little sad to have left heaven, but since then I have used this brief gift to help motivate me to do good things during the time I have remaining in this life, in the hope of returning to heaven when the time is right.

* * *

One other curious thing happened the day of my first hip replacement surgery – I sort of died. I had been taken to my room in the ward where I would spend the rest of the week recovering from the surgery, and I was naturally in a lot of pain. The nurse decided to give me an i.v. injection of morphine. As she gave me the injection, I began to feel nauseous. I vomited, but then also began to feel really weird. Next, as I have been told, my eyes rolled back in my head, and my heart stopped. The nurse hit the code blue button, and began shaking me and calling my name. Very quickly my heart kicked back into action, and I began to wake up, but in a state of confusion. I remember being very annoyed with the nurse, and wondering why the hell she was shaking me so hard! Then I slowly realized that there had been a lapse in time, and the code blue was still sounding. I had worked in a hospital, so I knew that meant a life-threatening emergency. I began to realize the code blue was for me, and that's why the nurse was calling my name as she shook me.

As she asked me if I was alright, and I said I didn't know but I felt OK, the room quickly filled with medical staff rushing to answer the code blue. I noticed the anesthesiologist from before surgery, and when she looked around at a room full of alert people, she asked who was the code blue. I raised my hand, and said something like "I think that would be me." She asked if I was OK, I said I thought so, and she began talking to someone else. It was all very strange, but apparently no big deal. I didn't get any more morphine, and it didn't happen again.

* * *

So I moved on to hip replacement number two, and then began the long recovery for both hips. In a couple of months I began teaching Taekwondo again, walking around class with a cane. Then I slowly began training myself. It was a steady process of getting better, then working harder, then hurting and needing to back off. But each two steps forward led to only one step back, and I steadily improved. The most noticeable improvement was that I was able to move my right leg in ways that were impossible before the second surgery. However, not having ever been particularly flexible, I was extremely tight after the standard procedure of protecting the entire hip region after such major surgery.

About a year after the second surgery, I left the Taekwondo school. At the same time, largely by coincidence, I learned about a new school opening that was going to offer Brazilian Jiu Jitsu and Muay Thai. I had been very interested in both of these martial arts, so I began attending the school. I was terribly nervous that I was going to have a dislocated hip in no time. However, Brazilian Jiu Jitsu has helped to both stretch and strengthen my hips, and Muay Thai keeps me active in the punching and kicking I was used to in Taekwondo (though there are also many differences).

I have now competed in my first Brazilian Jiu Jitsu tournament, and I have been talking to my Muay Thai instructor about something like a K-1 tournament (restrained kick boxing). I must be an idiot! I am 51 years old, with two artificial hips, and I'm new at this stuff. But I like it, and I'm not afraid to take a beating. And there is always the slim possibility that I might win something. I do try.

* * *

On the more sensible side, I became interested in martial arts programs for people with physical disabilities. Several things came together at the same time, in another one of those amazing coincidences that Carl Jung would refer to as synchronicity. As described in an earlier chapter, synchronicity is the theory that when certain events occur together in time, without any causal relationship, they are nonetheless connected by something greater, something spiritual (e.g., Tao, or God's plan).

I was looking for a nice cane, and learned about the Cane Masters International Association (CMIA), founded by Grandmaster Mark Shuey, Sr. They not only offer a wide variety of custom canes, but they also have an organized self-defense program. I had purchased a book by Shawn Withers, a stroke survivor, who along with his wife runs Natural Motion Martial Arts in Maine. They teach Broken Wing Kenpo, a style they developed, and Andrea Withers has developed an approach to teaching martial arts to people with physical disabilities called the C.R.I.T.I.C.A.L. Approach™. I also learned about the International Disabled Self-Defense Association (IDSA), founded by Master Jurgen Schmidt, which offers a program called Defense-Ability for people who use wheelchairs.

During this same period of time, my interests in Buddhism, meditation, and mindfulness had been growing steadily. I had taken some classes at the Barre Center for Buddhist Studies in Massachusetts, and attended a Vipassana retreat next door at the Insight Meditation Society (10 days of noble silence, 12 hours of meditation a day).

Since my hip problems had limited my abilities in Taekwondo, I was naturally interested in the spiritual aspects of martial arts, including their largely Buddhist/Taoist tradition. All I needed was the time necessary to devote myself to some serious study. As it turns out, I had never taken a sabbatical. At Lansing Community College, we are eligible for sabbatical after six years of teaching. After 7, 8, 9 years, people kept asking me why I hadn't taken one. I said I didn't have an idea worthy of sabbatical. Considering what passes for a sabbatical around this place, my concerns seemed rather pointless, but I have too much integrity to take a sabbatical just for the sake of taking one. Now I had a reason, and the possibility of a sabbatical leave offered the time I would need. So after 12 years at the college, I applied for a sabbatical.

In January, 2009, I began my sabbatical to study the psychological and spiritual aspects of martial arts programs for people with physical disabilities. For the first two months I was recovering from my second hip replacement surgery. I worked steadily on my literature review and began writing. In February I went to the Barre Center and attended several weekend classes over a two week period. During the week, I spent time studying and writing in their library. They were gracious enough to have granted my request for a self-study project, so I was able to stay at the center.

50

It was only a 3-hour drive to Natural Motion Martial Arts in Maine, and Shawn and Andrea were nice enough to set up a special day for me to take the C.R.I.T.I.C.A.L. Approach™ course and train in Shawn's special style of cane self-defense called Cane~Dao (Shawn is also a Canemaster, through the CMIA).

After returning home, I continued writing and studying the CMIA's American Cane System. I also began studying Defense-Ability. In June, I traveled to North Carolina to study with Master Schmidt of the IDSA. In July, my son Samuel and I drove to Nevada for both a road trip and a chance to train with Grandmaster Shuey. Although it took a while to complete the necessary teaching hours and some other requirements, as I had proposed in my sabbatical application, I eventually completed certification in the C.R.I.T.I.C.A.L. Approach™, as a program administrator in Defense-Ability, and earned black belts in Defense-Ability and the American Cane System. In the midst of all this, I also earned my 2nd Dan (2nd degree black belt) in Taekwondo. I also visited programs in Chicago, Illinois and London, Ontario, published an article in *The Journal of Asian Martial Arts*, and wrote a book entitled *Psychological and Spiritual Factors in Martial Arts Programs for People with Physical Disabilities*.

Of course, none of this would mean a dang thing if that was the end of the story. So, here comes another synchronicity event. But first, a brief aside.

* * *

Last night, May 17th, 2010, I went to Muay Thai and was then going to stay for my first no gi submission wrestling class. I am also trying to lose some weight in preparation for my first Brazilian Jiu Jitsu tournament next month. I hadn't eaten much all day, and we were working out pretty hard in the Muay Thai class. By the end I was exhausted. I should have had enough sense to just quit, but I needed to start working on take-downs for the up-coming tournament, so I stayed for the next class.

Well, it was just pathetic. I had no energy. In addition to not having eaten much, I was seriously dehydrated from the first class (despite drinking water during class). We did some warm-ups, and then started working on take-downs, the very thing I needed to work on. But I just didn't have any energy. I soon realized that I was probably going to get hurt, and I really needed to leave class. So I sat for a while and watched. I figured I could still learn by watching.

I often say that the advantage of being older than everyone in class, by a lot, is that I don't feel any pressure. The Buddhist perfection of equanimity, which I am working to incorporate into my life, as well as mindfulness, both help me to face and accept the realities of my age and physical condition. But the truth is, I still get embarrassed a little bit. I don't want to be old, and disabled, and out of shape, and just plain tired. I want to be able to wrestle with 20- and 30-somethings, despite being 51, tired, dehydrated, and just plain spent. I know it's silly, but whatcha gonna do?

I went home. I'm not completely stupid.

* * *

After returning to LCC from sabbatical, I was telling our department coordinator about what I had been up to, and what some of my plans were regarding giving some talks on campus about my sabbatical and finishing the book I was writing. She told me that she had been to a meeting with our Business and Community Institute (BCI), and they were looking for new projects. My interests might fit well with theirs, so she put me in touch with one of the BCI employees.

I met with a couple of people from BCI, and they were amazed. They had been working on a project for the newly formed Capital Area Business Leadership Network Disability Council. And here I was thinking about offering self-defense programs for people with physical disabilities. Before I knew it, I was a member of the Disability Council, I was developing a course to be offered jointly by them and by LCC's BCI, and I had established my own business: Real-Life Self-Defense, LLC.

After presenting the outline of the course we were interested in offering, a vice president for Peckham, a company that specializes in hiring people with disabilities, came up to talk with me. She wanted to know if I would be interested in offering the program at her company, whether the Disability Council/BCI course worked out or not. I said I would be happy to. Well, things are going very slowly, especially with the state of the economy in Michigan right now, but this project remains in the works. And that isn't all.

One day I was at a council meeting hosted by Peckham, and one of their employees was giving a talk that day. He saw the Taekwondo jacket I was wearing, and he had trained in that same style some 30 years earlier. It turns out he had been at the school where my instructors had also trained before starting our school. And he just happened to know of a new Brazilian Jiu Jitsu school that was about to hold its open house. That's right; this is where I train now. I also plan to start offering the American Cane System and Defense-Ability classes there, either as a starting point, or as a follow up to the program we are still planning at his company.

Many great names in the fields of psychology and psychiatry, including Carl Jung, Elisabeth Kübler-Ross, and Carl Rogers talked about how often they encountered things which defied scientific explanation. It becomes increasingly difficult to dismiss these spiritual occurrences out-of-hand. Perhaps there will someday be a scientific explanation for synchronicity, or perhaps after we die it will become all too clear.

* * *

As mentioned in an earlier chapter, I previously noted the close correspondence between ancient martial arts codes of conduct and the six core virtues identified by Martin Seligman and Christopher Peterson. Perhaps it should not be surprising to see a correspondence between ancient martial arts codes of conduct and the core human virtues. The young men of the Ksatreya clan in ancient India, those who joined the P'ungwollto in ancient Korea (which included the hwarang), and Japanese samurai trained in Bushido, were all being prepared for more than just combat. They were being trained to be wise, moral, and capable leaders for their countries. As such, they had to be men of character. Aside from military leaders, there were also the monks, those responsible for ensuring the spiritual development and guidance of society.

The traditional emphasis of martial arts on values, integrity, self-control, philosophy, history, spirituality, etc., can help an individual martial artist become a better person. For example, consider the tenets of Taekwondo: courtesy, integrity, perseverance, self-control, and indomitable spirit. None of them directly refers to being a good fighter. They emphasize personal development in positive, constructive, and respectful ways. Of course, the martial arts are not the only pursuits in life which can help to develop virtue and strength of character, but they have a long tradition of intentionally doing just that.

Likewise, positive psychology is about far more than the martial arts. Actually, there is little mention of martial arts in the literature on positive psychology. But anything that contributes to an individual's well-being falls within the domain of positive psychology, and the popular concept of flow is often referred to in athletic competition.

* * *

Let us also consider, once again, Maslow's hierarchy of needs, which begins with four deficiency needs (physiological, safety, belonging, and esteem needs) and culminates in the being need of self-actualization. Martial arts schools which focus on fighting alone address only deficiency needs. Learning how to fight can certainly enhance one's safety, and provide a role within the group. A good fighter may even enjoy enhanced self-esteem and the esteem of others. But positive approaches to either psychology or martial arts, such as the psychological concept of self-actualization, seek something more that can enhance one's life and the lives of others. It may well be something related to the emphasis we find in the writings of existential psychiatrists and psychologists. Both Viktor Frankl and Rollo May emphasized the need to find meaning in one's life. As both men faced death, in the Nazi concentration camps for Frankl and in a sanitarium after being diagnosed with tuberculosis for May, these men recognized that those people who still found meaning in their lives were the ones most likely to survive.

It's interesting for me to consider how the martial arts have provided meaning in my own life. It is helping me to stay fit, lose weight, and meet new people. The connection with mindfulness of body and accepting my physical limitations is also helping to lower my blood pressure. My martial arts training also provides a surprising way to connect with some of my younger students at the college, whether they practice martial arts or not. It tells them I'm not just someone who, as a professor, likes to read and write books. It lets them know that I value physical activity just as much as mental activity. In other words, it helps to show my students, and my children, that I am trying to be a well-rounded person.

* * *

OK, this chapter has gone in some interesting directions: from surgery to synchronicity to positive psychology. How does this all fit together? In order to keep myself busy and physically fit I train in Muay Thai and Brazilian Jiu Jitsu. I also teach the American Cane System, and I am trying to set up Defense-Ability classes. My involvement in the martial arts follows a traditional path, one which incorporates meditation and mindfulness. Thus, my interests in Yoga, Buddhism, Taoism, and Christianity are complemented by my physical training. In addition, I view my work with people who have physical disabilities as more than just work, it is community service as well.

But it goes even deeper. I am a psychology professor, and I am scheduled to teach a positive psychology class in the next academic year. I will be incorporating my experiences into the typical academic material associated with positive psychology, and trying to convey to my students that this can become a complete way of life. Just as Carl Rogers strove to move beyond just helping people with psychological disorders to become normal, we can all strive for self-actualization. This is more than just being normal, it achieves well-being. Even the most well-adjusted, psychologically healthy people can be something more. Those who practice Yoga and Buddhism use terms such as enlightened. I certainly do not consider myself to be there yet. I am far too attached to such worldly things as the ex-wife I still love with all my heart. But I am working on accepting the end of our marriage, and feeling compassion for her as she strives to find whatever it is she is looking for in her life, and that helps me continue forward in my own life. So it all comes together in my belief systems, my career, my physical training, my community involvement, and my whole personal life.

* * *

I am going to end this chapter with three entries on a recent event that brings my martial arts training, my physical disability, and positive psychology together. It was my first Brazilian Jiu Jitsu tournament: the 2010 Hoosier Open in Indianapolis, Indiana. I had only been practicing BJJ for 3 ½ months, a very short time to learn the basics of this challenging style, and I do NOT have a grappling background (like many people who practice BJJ).

* * *

It is about 8:00 in the evening on June 11th, 2010, and I am relaxing in a hotel room in Indianapolis. I am hungry! Tomorrow I will be competing in my first Brazilian Jiu Jitsu tournament. I had to decide whether or not to lose the weight necessary to make it into the Super Heavyweight class. If I didn't, I would have to be in the unlimited class, and I could end up fighting someone 300, or even 400, pounds. So I finally got serious about losing some weight, which was part of the plan associated with this book. In order to make weight I needed to get down to 215 pounds. This morning I weighed 211.5 pounds. I am down over 20 pounds since January.

Despite making weight, I am still concerned about competing in a BJJ tournament with my artificial hips. I was never very flexible, and I am less flexible now and the muscles in my hips tend to respond slowly. At Magic BJJ everyone has been pretty good about watching out for my hips. I have steadily improved in flexibility, strength, and quickness. I will never be 100%, but how many guys 51 years old are still 100% of what they were at 25? Unfortunately, again, the oldest age group for the tournament is 41 years old and above. So I still might face people 10 years younger than me.

The head of our school, Matt Linsemier, worked with his coach, Ryan Fiorenzi, on some hip-friendly techniques to help me with what I anticipate will be the most challenging aspect of my fights: getting from my feet to the ground. I suppose there is a chance I will get thrown aggressively on one of my hips, but if not, I hope to gain an advantage even if I have to pull guard. That's what we worked on, and I have had some success with the techniques in class. However, in class we start rolling (the term for sparring in BJJ) from our knees. So tomorrow will be different than usual, and I will be competing against strangers. Maybe I'm crazy, but I will go ahead and do my best.

And then I decide how soon I have a nice big meal, if I feel like I deserve it based on my performance. Of course, I hope to continue losing weight, but I think I will deserve at least one good meal.

* * *

It is now Sunday afternoon, June 13th, the day after the tournament. It was quite an experience. I have competed in Taekwondo tournaments before, but the main difference is that BJJ tournaments only have the fights. So, rather than forms in the morning and sparring in the afternoon, I had to wait all day for the Senior Adult Super Heavyweight group to be called. And I do mean all day. The school owner's son is 16 years old, considered a junior. We had to be there at 8 am for his weigh-in. My group was schedule for noon weigh-in, and 2 pm competition. I didn't fight until around 4 pm.

I had gotten my weight right where I wanted it, but I had to eat very little on Friday, and then I couldn't really eat or drink on Saturday morning until after weigh-in. There were some other white belts in our school, so we all had to wait until noon. When one of the higher ranking students had a fight it kept our minds occupied, but we were all pretty happy to finally get the weigh-in out of the way. The limit for super-heavyweight was 221 pounds with the gi on, and my gi weighs about 5 pounds. My official weight was 217.6 pounds, and the snack that followed was great. Of course, at that point you can't eat too much, because you are going to be fighting, so I had a Nutri-Grain bar and a banana, and some G2 Gatorade.

When the time finally came to fight, it turned out there were only 2 of us in each of the weight classes for senior men, and the tournament was double elimination. That meant we had to fight the same person best 2 out of 3 falls. My opponent was probably close to the full 10 years younger that he could be, a little taller than me, more experienced (he had stripes on his belt, I did not), and *very* strong. When we first locked up he stiff-armed me, something I hadn't experienced yet, and first tried to yank me forward and then tried to shove me back. I stood my ground both times, and began trying for the underarm collar grab my coach Matt had worked on with me. I was able to achieve the underarm grab and was just about to pull guard when he pulled guard and immediately swept me. *And then he grapevined me!*

The grapevine is a move where you intertwine your legs with your opponent's legs and stretch your opponent's legs far apart. The last time it was done to me in class I yelled "Stop" and immediately tapped out. As I said, I am not flexible, and this is not a good position for my hips. This time I was mindful of the experience, and the fear that came with it. There was no pain, so I continued to fight. I heard Matt tell me to straighten out my legs, and I tried. My opponent was simply the superior fighter. We grappled for a while, and then he went for one of my favorite moves, the Americana. Again

I heard Matt tell me to keep my elbow down, to fight his attempt at reaching his hand through and gaining the Americana. Again my opponent was superior. He locked up the Americana, twisted my arm, I felt pressure in my elbow, then pain, and I tapped out. The first fall had gone to my opponent.

We were allowed to rest while some other competitors had their matches, and then were called back to the mat. When the second match started my opponent tried to stiff arm me again, but I fought his hand off (actually with a Muay Thai style block). We got close to each other, and I tried to work for the underarm collar grab again, but he fought that off and created separation between us. For that instant, we had both attempted what had worked at the beginning of the first match, and we had both fought off what our opponent wanted to do. It is this mental game that I still love. Indeed, since this is something I can still do well, I now love it even more than the actual fighting. Then he shot for a double leg takedown, and was successful. My first thought was that he would attempt a grapevine again, but he was in position for the even more dominant position of mounting me. I quickly fought for half-guard position and achieved it. We both then went to work. I attempted to get a choke, he fought it off and attempted a choke of his own, which I fought off. He then started to work for mount again, and I used the opportunity to try sweeping him. I was almost successful, and I swept him off and down to his side. But he was able to recover before I could complete the sweep, since my hips still react slowly, and he came back into mount. I then tried the upa move in order to buck him off. He went a little too far forward to keep his weight on me, and I attempted to escape out the back door (basically going under his butt and coming out behind him). Once again, however, he recovered quickly and locked me in place with his leg. The failure of this final attempt to escape left him in high mount, and knew I was in trouble. He decided to attempt an Americana again, and he quickly got my right arm. In reaction, I rolled to my right, lowering my arm to the mat and putting my weight on my upper arm so he could not twist it. I tried to get hold of my right hand with my left, but he shifted his body weight on my hips and flattened me out. That's bad in BJJ! He twisted, I hurt, and I tapped out. He had won his 2 out of 3 falls, and my first Brazilian Jiu Jitsu tournament was over.

* * *

Believe it or not, I am a little surprised at what a positive experience this tournament was. And that positive experience is not just a matter of equanimity or mindfulness. It is not just one of those trite expressions like I am a winner just for getting out there to compete at my age with two artificial hips. It was positive in a variety of other ways, including the fact that I accomplished both of the goals I had set for myself.

First, I wanted to survive getting from the standing start down to the mat in once piece, still able to continue the fight. I accomplished that goal in different ways in each match. Second, I wanted to work some of the things Matt and I had specifically planned, as well as some of the basics we routinely study in class. I was able to do both, and some of it as a result of listening to Matt's coaching while the match was happening. I never expected to win, and my opponent was clearly superior (though, of course, we didn't know that beforehand). So winning or losing had nothing to do with what I wanted to accomplish. I walked out of the tournament at the end of the day (a goal in and of itself) knowing that I had been successful in terms of my reasonable goals.

Corey Ottgen and Travis VanKirk, two members of the school who have also helped me, wanted everyone to stop at the Waffle House on the way home and have dinner together. When we got there, they told me that everyone else had decided to just go straight home. So the three of us had dinner together, and we all ordered waffles (Corey had chocolate chip waffles), eggs, meat (bacon for me), hash browns, toast, and soda (Travis and I had root beer). It was amazing how fast we ate while still carrying on a conversion.

As we were leaving, Corey really surprised me. He thanked me for breaking bread with them. Those were his words, "breaking bread." You don't hear too many people use that phrase, especially outside of church. It added a personal touch to our camaraderie, and it meant a lot to me. This is something that is an ancient, fundamental aspect of the martial arts. We often think of it as either respect or friendship, but in the martial arts the two are blended together in a unique way. This is true not only for members of your own school, but also for your opponents from other schools. At the end of my two matches, I told my opponent and the referee about my hips, and that I teach martial arts to other people with physical disabilities. They were amazed, and gave me great encouragement. They both wanted pictures with me, and the referee said he would be telling all his friends about it. Between that moment of camaraderie with my opponent and the referee, and breaking bread with Corey and Travis, losing my matches seems so irrelevant. I came home in a very, very good mood.

Will I compete in another Brazilian Jiu Jitsu tournament? We'll see. Probably. But it wasn't easy, and I won't make any promises. Not to myself, and not to anyone else. I'll know if it feels right the next time the team is planning to attend a tournament. If it doesn't feel right to compete, I will be attending with my camera, and working on my indoor action photography.

God and Hell

I would like to address a couple of topics which I think profoundly affect my life. I believe in God, and I believe in hell. What's more, I know what hell is, and where it is. You may disagree with me, but here is what I believe.

* * *

For many years I conducted biomedical research. With a Ph.D. in Physiological Psychology, I spent most days at work performing surgery, recording the activity of single neurons in the rat brain, and administering experimental drugs in order to advance our understanding of Tourette Syndrome, Parkinson's Disease, and schizophrenia. I was pretty good at research. I had a major federal research grant, I helped to refute one line of research which involved a Nobel laureate (unfortunately so, because it was a very promising line of research with safe medications), and I really stepped up with a series of studies on the effects of anesthesia in the brain systems being studied by people in my field.

Many scientists are atheists. And many of those atheists think that scientists must be atheists, because there is no scientific evidence for God, and there likely never will be. I'm sure God likes it that way. For me, the more I learned about how the brain works, the more I learned about cellular physiology and biochemistry and genetics (I was a co-author on one genetics paper), the more I learned about what awesomely complex and fascinating biological organisms that we are, the more I noticed an *absolute lack of anything that I would call life*. Life is so much more than the collective processes of biological matter. Even if we accept that consciousness is an emergent phenomenon of the collective activity of the billions of neurons in the brain, we still cannot explain things like love, lost love, wonder, curiosity, fun, or contentment.

I will admit that evolutionary psychologists have gone to amazing lengths to explain things like laughter in terms of their evolutionary advantage. If I'm not mistaken, I think we have Jaak Panksepp to thank for some of the laughter research, an evolutionary biologist I have met a few times over the years (though I doubt he remembers who I am). Yet, what evolutionary advantage is there for me to acknowledge their contributions? I will not have any more children, so I cannot pass on again any selective advantages.

This leaves me with only one conclusion: life itself, the true essence of life, is the spark of divinity within each of us that emanates from God. Call it a soul, atman, spirit, whatever you like. It elevates us from the biochemistry of the primordial goo from which we evolved. That's right, I am an unabashed supporter of evolution. I believe that is how God created us, or allowed our creation to occur, or observed our creation occurring... And when the time was right, he blessed us with that tiny spark of divinity that gave life to the world, and I imagine many other worlds throughout the universe.

* * *

Before turning to hell, let me say a little more about why I believe in God, or Tao, or at least *something* greater than the physical universe. I will clearly be taking off my scientist hat now, and probably giving fits to theoretical physicists, but I challenge them to *absolutely prove* that I am wrong here. I know they can't, no scientist ever absolutely proves anything, so it's an easy challenge.

I believe in the Big Bang theory of the creation of the universe. However, this means two things. First, something existed before the universe, and second, the universe is expanding into something. Now I know there are cosmological theories which explain away these fundamental problems, but they just don't make common sense. Crazy as it may sound, there are also theories that there are many other universes, but they all occupy the same space as ours! Exotic experiments have challenged Einstein's theory that nothing can exceed the speed of light and have apparently violated Heisenberg's uncertainty principle. Scientists have even created the first cloaking devices, though they are very, very limited. I don't quite understand why some of these theoretical physicists think that "God" is a stranger idea than some of the things they are proposing and studying themselves.

If God existed before the Big Bang, and He is what the universe is expanding into, then He would certainly defy any scientific explanation. But having something greater than the whole universe, which gave rise to the Big Bang and is the domain within which our universe is expanding, is simply common sense. Don't call it God if you don't want to, but I will.

* * *

Hell! For those of us who believe in it, hell brings up frightening images and fears. A lake of fire that can never be quenched, often associated with the center of the earth (far deeper than a grave). Complete separation from God. Total darkness. Reincarnation as a creature with such limited consciousness that enlightenment is countless lifetimes away. I thought of a way to combine such varied ideas with a question I have always had about evolution. Why do some organisms evolve in environments so harsh that the only thing you can do is survive, and nothing else? For example, tiny worms that live in glaciers, or sulfur eating bacteria that live near volcanic steam vents at the bottom of the ocean.

Here is what I came up with: hell is being reincarnated as a sulfur eating bacteria living by one of those volcanic steam vents at the bottom of the ocean. Think about it. Many Eastern cultures believe that if you live an evil life, due to your karma, you will be reincarnated as an organism that is countless lives away from enlightenment. Modern Christians often talk about sin as that which separates you from God, and hell as the complete absence (unawareness?) of God. What is less sentient than a single-celled organism? We hear descriptions of a lake of fire, which cannot be quenched. Sound like liquid, molten rock, pouring out of the earth, into the greatest body of water there is? It is dark there, and very cold as well if you move away from the lava. And why would anything want to exist there? Sure, maybe it just happened by chance billions of years ago, when there wasn't any other life, or any hospitable land. But maybe, just maybe, God created bottom-dwelling, sulfur eating, roasted by lava, crushed under intense pressure, ridiculously separated from the rest of the world bacteria as a way to punish people who lived sinful lives.

Something to think about, isn't it?

* * *

So I believe in God, and I believe in hell. I think that makes it essential that each of us does as much good as we can in this life. We need to be compassionate, we need to help others, we need to make the world a better place. Many spiritual leaders have said that the best way to make the world a better place is to begin with yourself. You can only control yourself. So strive to make yourself a better person. Strive to self-actualize, or attain enlightenment, whatever you want to call it, or however you want to go about it. There isn't just one way to do it, you need to find the best way for you. But you need to do it. Because if there is no God, if there is no life after this one, it would really be a shame to waste this life without it having had any meaning.

Thanksgiving Day, 2009

Thanksgiving has always been an important holiday for me. This Thanksgiving, however, was unique. For the first time in my life, I spent Thanksgiving alone. If I hadn't gone to the video store to rent a movie, I wouldn't have spoken to anyone, all day long. So, what do I have to be thankful for? A lot really, so let's take a closer look at this day.

The reason that Thanksgiving means a lot to me is that I can trace my heritage directly to the Mayflower. Since this line of my ancestry goes to John Howland, through him and the family which remained in England at the time, I have some very notable, though very distant, relatives. These notable relatives include U. S. Presidents Franklin D. Roosevelt, George H. W. Bush, George W. Bush and Continental Congress President Nathaniel Gorham. Among the descendants of John Howland's brothers are U. S. Presidents Richard Nixon and Gerald Ford, and British Prime Minister Sir Winston Churchill. When I was young, this history and these distant relations were a source of great pride. It helped me feel important, especially when we celebrated Thanksgiving in New England, where I grew up.

Something strange, however, was the reasoning behind this source of pride and the feelings of connection to a family. My family was never close. My parents played my sister, brother, and I against each other. More often than not, my brother and sister wanted nothing to do with my father, but I was always defending him. I tried to get them to understand that no matter what had happened between our parents, he was still our father. This often led to me being taken advantage of, something I would become good at throughout my life. Thanksgiving was one of the holidays we would go to visit my father's parents in New Jersey. I loved my grandmother Kelland dearly, and also had a lot of fun with my Uncle Larry and Aunt Betsy. But the ride from Massachusetts to New Jersey was not much fun.

My father had an MG. It was a small, 2-seat sports car. With three children, there wasn't room for us in the car. So, my older brother and my sister got to share the seat. I sat on the floor under the dashboard! It takes a while to drive from Massachusetts to New Jersey. I honestly don't remember how many times this happened, but I accepted it as my responsibility. I was the one strong enough to deal with this abuse. I was the one who cared enough about family to allow my brother and sister to enjoy the drive. It is one of the most salient memories of my childhood, and despite some degree of resentment, it is a source of personal pride.

As an adult, living in Michigan, and being married to someone with a very large family, Thanksgiving took on another interesting meaning. The Detroit Lions play football on Thanksgiving. So there was always a large crowd around the television watching the game. Win or lose (and for years now the Lions have been one of the worst teams ever), enjoying the game and the big gathering of family was something I enjoyed.

This year I went for a hike on Thanksgiving. It was chilly, and I hadn't been on a very long hike since well before I had my hips replaced. While hiking, I heard an occasional shot from deer hunters off in the distance. I had been squirrel hunting with my son John recently, and he has been looking forward to deer hunting next year. I am not really into hunting, I would much rather go fishing, but I promised him I would go with him next year. I doubt it will be on Thanksgiving Day, because it is important to me that he remain close with my ex-wife's family. Indeed, during our mediation, I gave her the right to have our children with her on every holiday. I could see no good reason they should spend the day sitting around with me, being depressed and bored. I can see them other days. Our relationship does not depend on the date on the calendar; it depends on how much we care about each other.

So I hiked through the woods, chilly and lonely, thinking about the sacrifice I had made, sacrifices I have been making all my life. I was alone under the dashboard of the MG because my father didn't care. I was alone on a trail in the woods because, as a father, *I do care!*

* * *

Mindfulness comes at a cost. Many people would rather deny reality, or explain it away in some irrational manner. It can be a challenge to both recognize one's personal reality and accept it with all its flaws.

I would like to add some more thoughts on giving thanks here, based on some things that happened in early June 2010. I'd had a very busy and productive week, getting some very important things accomplished. I finished a major revision of the index for my textbook, in anticipation of having it published by KendallHunt and getting it out on the national market. I set up my online summer classes, as well as my ex-wife's class (which I still set up for her each semester). And then I did some important screening of applications for the search committee on which I had been serving as chair. As I was heading to my Muay Thai class on Friday, I should have been feeling pretty good, having gotten three major tasks accomplished. Instead, I became very depressed, almost overwhelmingly depressed. It was the kind of depression you really feel physically.

For a second I was frightened by how powerfully this wave of depression overcame me, but almost as quickly I became mindful of my feelings. I observed the depression, and the fear, and found them interesting. My mindfulness immediately dispelled the fear, but the depression was clear and present. Why? I began to examine my feelings, and explore their roots. Within a minute or so it was all very clear. For about 25 years, whenever interesting things were happening in my career, I would talk to my best friend about them. Especially with something like being on a search committee, or the accomplishment of getting a book ready for publication, and the fact that my best friend was also in the field of psychology, we were really able to understand what we were each going through (the good and the bad). Unfortunately, my best friend had divorced me. And no one could possibly take her place, at least not in the same way, since we had begun our careers together and intertwined our lives with those careers.

The next morning I continued to contemplate what it really meant to have gotten divorced. What exactly changed in my ex-wife's life? As I see it, there were 2 major changes for her. First, I moved out of our house. Second, she didn't have to keep it a secret any longer that she had been dating. Both of these were good things for her. So what changed for me? I lost the woman I loved, and I lost my best friend. I had to leave my home. I have to struggle from paycheck to paycheck, since I am still paying half the mortgage and lots of child support. What made the situation even worse, is that I had to suffer from these losses not because of anything I did, but because I had been betrayed by the woman I loved, and because I would not fight her and end up dragging our children into the middle of our problems.

Now, how does this fit into a discussion of giving thanks? It has to do with what really hurts about the things I have lost. First, I lost the woman I loved. But she didn't love me, so it would be selfish of me to want her to stay. I sincerely hope she someday finds the kind of love I feel for her. It really is a wonderful feeling, despite the pain it ultimately led to. There is also the possibility that someday I will meet someone who actually does love me, though it is hard to imagine how I will meet someone. I am thankful that I had the opportunity to feel what it feels like to truly love someone, and to know that in spite of what has happened, I still feel that love. I know what undying love feels like, and I am glad I can feel it.

I had to leave my home, but the agreement we made gives me the opportunity to move back home in a few years, while our younger son is still in high school. So it may be home again. In the meantime, my small apartment, empty and all too often lonely, is still a roof over my head. Many people in this world, even here in the United States, as disgraceful as this may be, are homeless. When we use that word, "homeless," we aren't talking about how I feel right now. We are talking about people who actually don't have a roof over their head. I am thankful I am not in that situation, and I give thanks routinely for having a steady job.

Having a steady job also addresses the matter of money. Sure I struggle from paycheck to paycheck, but I get a steady paycheck. And the child support I pay is going to my children, because I care for them. And the money I pay for the mortgage on the house my ex-wife lives in expresses, in part, the compassion I feel for her, as I wonder if she will ever find what she is looking for. So I am thankful.

As for my ex-wife betraying me, well, I guess that's my side of the story. She may have a different perspective. I will have to meditate, and bring mindfulness to bear on those feelings. There really isn't any good way for a 23 year marriage to end.

So what is left? The reason my divorce hurts, the reason I was overwhelmed with depression, as I so often am, is that I lost my best friend of 25 years. My whole adult life, the entire householder stage, was intimately intertwined with one good friend. Now she is gone, and I never did anything to hurt that friendship. If I were an enlightened master, I could accept even this loss with equanimity. But I am not yet that far along the path. Indeed, according to the Vedas, I am just now at the point of starting along the path toward enlightenment. It gives me hope, but not quite enough solace. At least not yet.

So I give thanks. Thanks for what I have, and thanks for what I have *not* lost. I have 2 wonderful children, I have a fulfilling career, I have found a path that is helping me to accept all that has happened and to forge a plan for the future. I am thankful.

And yet, the future still seems challenging. The feeling that life is a challenge doesn't go away easily. But I can also be thankful that my emerging mindfulness is helping me to examine those feelings as well.

* * *

There is a passage in the *Tao Te Ching* about a person who knows enough is enough always having enough. There is also a saying that it isn't about having what you want, it's about wanting what you have. Wasn't the latter saying in a Cheryl Crow song? Anyway, Gotama Buddha taught that human suffering is about craving, or desire. It can be frightening how ungrateful some people are, how greedy they can be. Sure it's nice to have a few nice things, to be able to go out for nice dinner, or take an exciting trip. Just remember to be thankful when you can, and to be compassionate toward those who can't.

Perspective

As a college professor who has written a number of articles and books, as well as having reviewed many articles, book chapters, and even book proposals, I can't help but compare my own writing to things published by other people. This is especially true when those other people have not only done amazing things, but in some cases I have also had a chance to meet them. I just want to briefly introduce you to a few people whose stories I think you will find interesting.

* * *

Erik Weihenmayer is a famous mountain climber. He is a published author, including *Touch the Top of the World: A Blind Man's Journey to Climb Farther than the Eye can See* (2001, Dutton), he has been featured in films, and he gives many talks. That's how I met him quite a few years ago. He came to the Michigan Ice Fest, an annual gathering of ice climbers in Michigan's Upper Peninsula, which I used to attend every year. My climbing partner and I met Erik when he gave his first talk at Northern Michigan University. We got a chance to talk to him afterward, so the next day we knew each other as we all went out to the curtains, a popular ice climbing area. We spent the day climbing with Erik, while his dog spent the day looking for protected places to sleep behind the overhanging ice cliffs.

Watching Erik climb is really a pleasure, he is incredibly smooth as he climbs. He would reach up with his ice axe, feel the ice above him, and when he located just the right spot, he would draw his axe back and sink the tip beautifully into the ice. You couldn't tell at all that he is blind. That's right, Erik is blind. He lost his sight due to a rare medical condition. Somewhat by coincidence he was introduced to rock climbing, and climbing eventually became a very important part of his life. Not letting his impairment hold him back, he is one of a small number of people who have climbed the 7 summits, the highest point on each continent.

His dog, by the way, is no ordinary dog. He is a professional seeing-eye dog. That day, however, he got to spend most of his time either sleeping or being spoiled by the attention of all the climbers who came to the curtains.

* * *

Trevon Jenifer was the fourth child of a poor, single mother living in a ghetto outside of Washington, DC. He was also born without legs. However, thanks to his mother's support, and a step-father who helped provide a stable home, Trey's life steadily improved from that challenging beginning. He became active in wheelchair track and basketball. In high school, however, his step-father suggested that he try out for the wrestling team, the *regular* wrestling team. It was a challenge that Trey pursued whole-heartedly. In his senior year, he earned a 3rd-place finish in the Maryland state championships.

Trey went on to attend Edinboro College, where he joined the wheelchair basketball team. He was kind enough to answer the email I sent him a few years ago, while I was working on my personality textbook. He had done well in his first year of college, and although he missed wrestling, he was enjoying the success of Edinboro's wheelchair basketball team. Joined by a co-author and writer, Trey shared the story of his life through high school in *Trevon Jenifer: From the Ground Up* (2006, Sports Publishing LLC).

* * *

Grandmaster Mark Shuey, Sr. has black belts in Tang Soo Do, Tae Kwon Do, and Hapkido. He has won many martial arts awards, holds several instructor certifications, and has been inducted into numerous Halls of Fame. He first used the cane as a martial arts weapon in Hapkido, and in 2000 he established the Cane Masters International Association (CMIA). The CMIA offers a complete program in self-defense with the cane, as well as providing a source of high quality, customizable canes. I encourage you to visit www.canemasters.com; some of the unique canes they offer are simply fun to look at.

I learned about the CMIA while searching the internet for a nice cane, as my degenerating hips made it necessary for me to use one regularly. Although Grandmaster Shuey gives seminars all over the world, in the summer of 2009 my son Samuel and I drove to Nevada to meet with him at the CMIA headquarters. The training session was a requirement of earning my black belt in the American Cane System, which was finally completed in the spring of 2010.

The interesting thing about the cane is that it isn't just for people who have long-term difficulty walking. I had several serious football and track injuries when I was young, as well as the accident involving the horse that led to my hip replacements. As soon as I could get rid of those annoying crutches, I was using the cane I bought at O'Reilly's Pharmacy, where I worked in high school. As many people get older they begin using a cane. Thus, the cane is a self-defense weapon we might all want to train with, since each one of us may be using one someday.

* * *

I first met Shawn Withers through his book *Broken Wing: You can't quit. Not ever.* (2007, Mystic Wolf Press). In 2009, I had the pleasure of meeting Shawn and his wife Andrea in person at Natural Motion Martial Arts in Scarborough, Maine, where they specialize in providing martial arts training for people with physical disabilities. Sensei Shawn Withers is a stroke survivor, with significant left-side weakness. They both hold 2nd degree black belts in Shaolin Kenpo and black belts in O-Ki-Tao. Shawn is also a Canemaster in the CMIA system.

Finding that the adjustments he made to accommodate his physical challenges did not always work as desired, the Withers' developed a unique style, known as Broken Wing Kenpo. Broken Wing Kenpo blends a variety of styles, and is intended to be adapted to the abilities of each student. Sensei Andrea Withers also developed a program for training instructors who would like to work with people who are physically challenged (the term they prefer to use). When I took the C.R.I.T.I.C.A.L. Approach™ course I found it to be a comprehensive program providing guidelines for meeting with new students, planning their martial arts training, assessing and re-evaluating that plan, and making sure that the training is fun.

After taking the course, I spent a few hours training with Shawn and one of his assistant instructors, John Pratt. As we worked together I was impressed with Sensei Withers' true love for the martial arts and his quiet attention to whether my own disability would create any problems for me. I look forward to having an opportunity to meet them again. You can learn more about their school at their website: www.naturalmotionmartialarts.com.

* * *

I met Master Jurgen Schmidt in the summer of 2009, when I traveled to Asheville, North Carolina to test for my black belt in Defense-Ability and take his seminar for instructors. Master Schmidt established the International Disabled Self-Defense Association (IDSA) in 1996, and developed Defense-Ability for people who use wheelchairs. He has used one since an armed assailant shot him in the back. Recognizing an alarming increase in crimes against people with disabilities, he continued his own training in Combat Hapkido while also developing his own unique style.

The Defense-Ability program is available on DVD, and it can stand alone. In other words, no other martial arts experience is necessary. An important aspect of his instructor's program is addressing whether a new instructor realizes exactly what they are getting into. This is not easily answered, but an important step is thinking about this very problem. Then, only experience can really help to prepare and develop the would-be instructor. Information on Master Schmidt's programs can be found at the IDSA website: www.defenseability.com.

I recently read a fascinating book by Matthew Sanford entitled *Waking: A Memoir of Trauma and Transcendence* (2006, Rodale). The book was recommended by Kirsten Mowrey, my massage therapist. It sounded like a real feel-good book about triumphing over tragedy. It wasn't! Mr. Sanford offers a fascinating, albeit frightening, description of the many medical procedures he underwent after suffering a broken back in a terrible car accident. That accident claimed the lives of his father and sister, making his recovery all the more difficult due to the added emotional trauma. Later, he broke his neck, and then his femur (the large bone in the upper leg). And yet, Mr. Sanford now teaches Yoga!

So you see, it was meant to be something of an uplifting book, but there was a lot more detail about the medical challenges following a severe, acquired paralysis than I expected. And then there was the final chapter in the book. That chapter really surprised me, and I strongly encourage you to read it. It really spoke to me, as I know a little something about his experience.

* * *

Another fascinating book I highly recommend is Andrew Potok's *A Matter of Dignity* (2002, Bantam Books). This book contains a series of interviews with people who work with others who have physical disabilities. Some of the individuals have physical disabilities themselves, while others do not. One chapter covers the Seeing Eye headquarters in Morristown, NJ. When I was a baby we lived near Morristown, and my grandparents lived there. My mother told me that when I was first born she would sometimes push my baby carriage around downtown Morristown while the dog trainers were working with the Seeing Eye dogs. I really wish I could remember that, but I was far too young. Other chapters include an interview with a man who specializes in making prosthetic limbs, and the creator of the JAWS computer program that converts Microsoft Windows and internet searches into speech for people who are blind.

Plans for the Future

As I wrote the outline for this book, I immediately thought of one thing regarding the title of this chapter. Suicide! But I actually typed it as: Suicide?? The two question marks reflect my extreme confusion about both the topic of suicide and my feelings about suicide, intellectual feelings and personal feelings. There have been times in my life when I really was suicidal, but this is not one of those times. I think I am finally past the possibility of ever really being suicidal again, but I wonder. Many people say suicide is an act of cowardice, but I think of it as comforting. It is the one thing in our lives we can seemingly control. The problem is, we don't get a do-over if we realize we made a mistake! And there is another important reality: we have control over our lives in another, much more important way.

Suicide is an illusory control. It ends your life, putting an end to your problems in this life, but what then? It certainly does not allow one to improve their life. I must admit that I admire the concept of ritual suicide, such as the Japanese practice of seppuku (more commonly known as hara-kiri), but even that only brings an end to one's life with dignity. If one focuses on self-development, or self-actualization, or self-realization, or enlightenment, then ending one's life is the ultimate failure, because you are absolutely ensuring that you will not become a better person. No matter how challenging life may seem, no matter how lonely and depressed you may be right now, no matter how difficult it may be to see a way past your problems, just focus on becoming a better person. That is something you can control, and no one can take that away from you. And if they try, just accept them for who they are, try to feel compassion for how desperate their need for control has become to them, and turn the other cheek.

* * *

Wednesday, June 2, 2010: It is an interesting day. I haven't been working on this book for a couple of weeks, because I got the copyediting back on my textbook. This will be the first version of my textbook published by KendallHunt, so it will get on the national market. It was a lot of detail work, so it was pretty mind-numbing. But now that it is done (I hope), I feel pretty good. I have other things to focus on, and not just this book.

I am training for my first Brazilian Jiu Jitsu tournament, which is now 10 days away. I have been doing pretty well lately, in both Brazilian Jiu Jitsu and Muay Thai, but I have been nervous about my hips. Last night my senior instructor, Matt Linsemier, worked with me on some takedowns that either pull guard with an advantage or lead immediately into a sweep. He had gone over the plan with his instructor, Ryan Fiorenzi (Michigan's first Brazilian Jiu

Jitsu black belt), and it seems like the plan will work pretty well for me. So now I can actually visualize how to be aggressive when the matches start, and that is a much better plan than just hoping to survive.

One minor problem that still remains, aside from my general lack of experience in "jits," is that I need to lose a little weight. If I don't make the 221 pound weight limit, I would have to fight in the unlimited weight class. So, I could actually fight someone 300 pounds or more. This morning I weighed 220 pounds, but you have to weigh in with your gi on. Jiu Jitsu gis are heavy, my weighs about 5 pounds. So I need to lose the weight of the gi, and a couple pounds more just to be comfortable. Of course, I am working hard this week, so losing the weight is just a matter of not pigging out this weekend.

Things are also looking up a little bit with the self-defense programs for people with physical disabilities. I have been teaching an American Cane System class for the Howell Parks & Recreation Department, and a member of the school where I train in jits and Muay Thai has been working on setting up some classes where he works (with people who are disabled). But, he doesn't have insurance. I told him that I have insurance for my company, but I'm not really using it because I have so few students. So, we might work together, and I'll start getting my money's worth out of my insurance policy. In addition, Magic Brazilian Jiu Jitsu, where we both train, is about to expand. I have talked to Matt and his wife/co-owner Amy about teaching classes in their school when they expand. It should be a great match, and it's wonderful how it all seems to be just falling right into place.

A few days after the tournament, I am heading out west with my son Samuel and one of his good friends. We don't really have a plan, but we are going to Death Valley, the Grand Canyon, and the meteor crater in Arizona. Other than that, we are just going to cruise around and see the sights. Should be fun!

* * *

So, here was a fairly simple something I had planned for the future: a road trip out west with my son Samuel. We took our first western road trip a year ago, so this summer's trip was our second tour of the country.

As I was training for my black belt in the American Cane System last year, one of the requirements I had to fulfill was a training session with either Grandmaster Shuey or another cane master. Although I had spent a little time training with cane master Shawn Withers when I took the C.R.I.T.I.C.A.L. Approach™ course developed by his wife Andrea, at that time I wasn't ready for my black belt. I wasn't able to find a seminar being held anywhere near Michigan, so I called the CMIA headquarters in Nevada. They suggested that I try contacting one of the cane masters in Minnesota, to which I suggested that I might just come out to Nevada and meet Grandmaster Shuey himself. I decided to drive, and I invited Samuel, who had recently gotten his learner's permit. It was a great opportunity for him to get in a lot of driving hours, and we headed off on our first road trip. For the first time, Samuel crossed the Mississippi and Missouri Rivers, the Rocky Mountains, the salt flats of Utah, and the high deserts of Nevada. We also went for a short hike in the mountains near Lake Tahoe.

A week before writing this, we returned from our second road trip. This summer we took along one of his friends, Aaron, who had never been out west (as Samuel had not been the summer before). We drove through Michigan, Indiana, Illinois, Missouri, Oklahoma, Texas, New Mexico, Arizona, Utah, Nevada and California. On the way home we came back through Nevada, Utah, Colorado, Kansas, Missouri, Illinois, Indiana, and Michigan. We visited the Petrified Forest National Park, the Arizona Meteor Crater, Sunset Crater Volcano and Wupatki National Monuments, and the north rim of the Grand Canyon. After stopping at the Gold and Silver Pawn Shop (where they film the hit TV show Pawn Stars), we went to Death Valley, and then went hiking on Wheeler Peak and toured Lehman Cave in the Great Basin National Park. On the drive home we crossed the canyon lands of Utah, the Rocky Mountains, the Missouri and Mississippi Rivers, and went up to the top of the Gateway Arch in St. Louis.

As wonderful as these sites were, the most exciting part of the trip was probably our brief sojourn across the panhandle of Texas. Samuel was pulled over for speeding! That first time getting pulled over can be pretty nerve-wracking. When the trooper asked Samuel for his license and the rental agreement for the car, Samuel said "Yeah." I smacked Samuel on the leg and told him to say "Yes, sir," and I told him to apologize and say that he didn't realize he was going quite so fast. I then told the trooper the same thing, and that I was resting and not really watching Samuel's speed that carefully. Actually, Samuel wasn't going very fast. The speed limit was 70 mph, and he had the cruise control set at 78 or 79. In Michigan, that's no problem. In Texas, with out-of-state plates, I guess that's not OK. Thankfully, the trooper just wrote Samuel a warning, and before long we were in New Mexico. But Samuel never went more than 3 or 4 mph over the speed limit after that.

I was really happy when Samuel said he was interested in going on our second road trip, and both he and Aaron seem very interested in another trip next summer. I am thinking about staying north. Possible sites include the Badlands and Black Hills of South Dakota (where I have been once), Devil's Tower in Wyoming, and Yellowstone National Park. If they don't want to go, I will probably go by myself. But I'm sure they will want to go, since we had such a good time this year.

73

* * *

Samuel with the warning he received from the Texas state trooper.

One thing that gets me very depressed is that I always seem to be helping other people, but no one is around to help me. This is especially true since my best friend for so many years has left me. As I ponder this situation, it is interesting to consider the reality of my perception. It is basically true, but the situation is a bit more complicated. I tend to be a leader and a doer. I teach for a living. I am someone others turn to, and that is just the way I like it. I enjoy being in control, especially when people acknowledge my ability to help them. As for myself, I don't need help very often, so there is no reason why anyone would be my go to person for help. It is also true that I have been helped somewhat, from time to time. But from early childhood I learned to be self-sufficient and independent, so it isn't easy for me to accept help.

Nonetheless, sometimes I feel very lonely and overwhelmed. And when that happens, when I feel like I really need someone to help me, there is no one there. This is the kind of thing you turn to a friend for, but I don't really have any friends. Sure I have nice acquaintances, but not the sort of friends I can turn to when I really need help. I don't even have a spiritual director at this point in my life, and I think that is who I might need the most.

So I get even more overwhelmed and sad when I realize, whether truly accurate or not (that doesn't matter, these are my feelings), that I am always giving, giving, giving, and never receiving any help in return. Recently I was in this state of mind, and I read something very interesting. Here is where I will quote someone, and it had to pretty meaningful for me to cite this passage after saying I didn't want to reference anything formally in this book. But this one really struck me:

> She kept following Ajaan Fuang's instructions until one day it occurred to her, "If I keep giving, giving, giving

like this, will I have anything left for myself?" When she told her doubts to Ajaan Fuang, he gave her a blank look for a second and then said, "Boy, you really can be narrow-hearted when you want to be, can't you?" Then he explained: "Good will isn't a thing, like money, that the more you give, the less you have. It's more like having a lit candle in your hand. This person asks to light his candle from yours, that person asks to light hers. The more candles you light, the brighter it is for everyone – including you."

(pp. 57-58; cited in *Awareness Itself: The Teachings of Ajaan Fuang Jotiko*, compiled & translated by Thanissaro Bhikku [Geoffrey DeGraff]. This is a free publication readily available on the internet from several different sources.).

* * *

The passage cited above is interesting not only because it addresses the issue of giving freely to others, and not only because I happened to read it at the time I was writing this, but also because I got a copy of *Awareness Itself* at a course taught by Ajaan Thanissaro (ajaan and bhikku are titles; when Mr. DeGraff became an ordained monk he took the title bhikku, and when he became a teacher he took the title ajaan; taking a different name is quite common in this tradition). It was a course on the ten perfections, and as I noted above, I have been working on the perfection of equanimity.

Equanimity involves a calm acceptance of life as it is, and events as they are. However, it is not meant to imply cold, emotionless detachment. I think the quote cited above helps to make that point. If you are doing things for others, and expect something in return, you are attached to what you are giving. Thus, you are not giving it freely, and you may feel that you are losing something of yourself in the process. However, if you give freely of yourself, with no expectation of payback and no sense of loss, then you have made the world a better place. That is good for you, whether or not you expected any good to come from your actions.

If someone needs my help, I should help them to the best of my ability. If I need help, and no one is there to help me, I should do the best I can alone. If the latter situation leads to feeling lonely, I can embrace my aloneness (a concept discussed by Anthony DeMello). Whatever the situation, one should simply accept life as it is, and do what they can to make the world a better place.

* * *

By the way, I am really annoyed by Facebook. I let my mother talk me into joining Facebook to keep in touch with her and some other family members. I also use it to check the schedule at Magic Brazilian Jiu Jitsu, so I really can't give it up now. But whenever I am feeling really depressed, or even when I come across something really awesome that I have read, no one comments on what I post on Facebook. Am I the one with the problem? Should I be more open to sharing all the meaningless drivel that most people post on Facebook. Sometimes it is funny, and sometimes it is informative (especially with schedules), but why is the good stuff I post ignored? I like deep, meaningful conversations about real issues, big issues, burning issues, existential/cosmological issues. Maybe I'm just too intense. Maybe I'm just too weird. Apparently I need to continue working on my equanimity.

* * *

I have come to the conclusion that I am a prophet. Either that or I am suffering from some very serious delusions, and must consider that I am quite mentally ill. I choose prophet, but not without giving the matter some lengthy consideration.

Throughout my life, even when I was a young child, I thought deeply about the meaning of religion and spirituality. When we had white bread and grape juice once a month at church, I wondered why we didn't bless the sacrament as Roman Catholics do. After all, if this was supposed to represent (or even *be*) the body and blood of Jesus Christ, shouldn't we have taken it more seriously? Many times I have picked up the Bible and read sections of it. I have read, and re-read the New Testament many times. Finally, I got a complete King James' Bible on tape and listened to it from beginning to end. But I want to emphasize that I *listened* to it. What is the message we are being given? I can tell you this, most self-proclaimed Christians, including many of our political and church leaders, are NOT Christian. The so-called "religious right" is an insidious group of Devil worshippers! There is good reason that one of Satan's names is "The Great Deceiver." And I have a few problems with the left-leaning media as well. Why do they talk about things like Christian Militia? There is no such thing as a Christian Militia – these people are Devil worshippers! What good is the First Amendment if the media isn't going to make sense when they talk about these things? Thank God for the Daily Show!

I love to challenge my students with religious pluralism and its implications. Most of them, if they have any religious tradition at all, are Christian. Jesus said that he was the only path to his Father. But, why does that mean you have to be Christian? Perhaps when a Buddhist achieves enlightenment, what really happens is that they meet Christ! So, a Buddhist, Daoist, Hindu, Muslim, Catholic, Protestant, shamanist, etc. who lives a

Christian life can enter heaven through Jesus Christ. It does not have to be impossible. In fact, anyone who claims to know exactly what is or is not acceptable to God, is claiming to know God's limitations. Sorry, but God doesn't have any limitations, least of all, the pettiness of the human minds of those who refuse to expand what little mind they have. What is required to live a Christian life? Love God (or Dao, or Great Spirit, etc.), and love your neighbor. It's that simple.

In order to be a prophet, however, one needs more than beliefs. One has to spread the message that has been revealed. Included in this concept is the belief that God has actually been revealing a message to me. This is where things get interesting. I have never been a saint. Nonetheless, God has revealed himself to me in some interesting ways. I'm not just talking about the synchronicity incidents, since they could be amazing coincidences. Neither am I talking about my trip to heaven, though that remains one of the great ways in which He has revealed Himself to me most recently. There have been other moments as well.

* * *

One day, when I was about 30 years old, I was driving down Rt. 96 in Michigan, approaching Livonia. The speed limit there is 70 mph, but in MI the police won't bother you as long as you don't over 80 mph. So, as usual, I had my cruise control set at 80 mph. I looked to my left out the window, and I saw a beautiful white dove flying alongside. As I admired the dove's beauty and grace, something amazing entered my mind. A dove cannot fly 80 mph (perhaps a racing pigeon can, but mourning doves max out about 55 mph). I quickly looked at my speedometer, and indeed I was going 80. I looked back to my left, and there was the dove, easily flying alongside. I suddenly realized this was no ordinary dove, it was the Holy Spirit letting me know that God was with me.

One day I was hiking in the Highland Recreation Area. This was not so long ago, so I was approaching this transition point in my life. I had been hiking mindfully, and was feeling very much in tune with nature. I stopped on a little bridge, and mindfully listened to the water passing underneath. On the upstream side, there were a bunch of rocks, and the water was gurgling and splashing over them. On the downstream side, the streambed was clear, and the water passed silently on its way. As I stood in the middle, it seemed as if the water was passing through me. All the noise, activity, and distraction of the splashing water upstream, representative of all the clutter that harasses us every day, was passing through me into silence. I realized that I had the ability to accept life as it is and be one with whatever comes my way. I slowly raised my face toward the sky, and the clouds parted. The warm sun struck my face, and I realized this was a gift from God. I experienced that moment

77

as something they call "touching your Buddha nature." Of course, in that instant of thought the clarity of my mind was broken. Still, the remainder of my walk was most enjoyable.

In yet another example of the cross-cultural nature of my experiences with divinity, and one perhaps more in keeping with whom I am as a person, I believe I met that great character of Native American religion: Coyote (the trickster). I was again walking in the Highland Recreation Area, a park close to where I live. This time it was winter, it was very cold, windy, and snowing steadily. I walked around a bend in the trail, and there before me was the biggest coyote I have ever seen. He was standing right in the middle of the trail, staring at me. I stopped, and looked him in the eye for a few seconds. As it seemed that neither one of us was going to move first, I did what seemed most natural at the time. I said, "Hi, Coyote." He slowly turned his head to the side, and then with a quick turn, simply vanished into thin air. I hike in the woods often, and do so at different times of day and in different seasons, so I have encountered many interesting animals. I have been snarled at by a mountain lion in New Mexico, bluff charged by a black bear in Virginia, and annoyingly harassed by a red squirrel for half a day in Maine. But this meeting with Coyote, and the way he vanished so suddenly and silently, was profoundly moving. Had I met my animal spirit guide?

* * *

So, believing since childhood that I had some special understanding of the value of the sacred, and having recognized numerous messages from God that He had some plan for me, what have I done about it?

I have always spoken openly about my faith, and an interesting variety of people have talked to me about it over the years. I often talk to my children about being a good person, and what that really means. In my classes I emphasize ethics and open-mindedness. I try to teach my children and my students to value learning about other people. This applies to individuals as well as cultures. I talk about trying to understand where another person is coming from. I challenge my students to think about the following situation. When you hear about a suicide bombing, in which many innocent people have been killed, do you feel compassion for the killer? Do you try to understand, and feel sad about, the conditions that led them to such a terrible act? So many people want to just condemn them and not think about the root causes of such horror. But if we can't feel compassion for everyone involved, including the terrorists, how can we resolve such a horrible state of affairs. Remember, terrorists are often misguided pawns of those who are truly evil. You don't see Osama bin Laden flying a jet into a building. No, he gets somebody else to do it. The Devil didn't raise no fool!

One of the reasons I enjoy teaching psychology is that I can cover these topics. Psychology is about life. In particular, I enjoy teaching personality, and I have published a personality textbook. As an academic topic, personality is the study of who we are, and how we became the person we are. I like to focus on who we can be next, and how we might choose to improve ourselves. It isn't easy, but the first step has to be thinking about it. If we don't make a choice to continue developing, and if we don't intentionally choose a healthy direction, the greed and defilements of life (I like the way Buddhists use the term *defilements!*) will surely lead us astray.

In my classes, in my textbook, in my relationships with other people (including my children), I try to teach others to open their eyes. See themselves for who they are. See the world for what it is. Recognize the evil agendas that so many false prophets have when they spread their lies. Spirituality is so important, but organized religion is so often a terrible thing. Never accept blind faith, but trust in yourself. Can you really trust yourself? You can if you have looked into your heart, and faced your own truth. That truth is that you are a child of God. If you believe that truth, if you listen to what that truth is telling you about how to live your life, you will do the right thing. That is what they call living an authentic life.

* * *

I was wandering around campus this morning, deep in thought. I was thinking about this book, as it was nearing completion. I was thinking about the interviews we were in the midst of for a position here at the college. I was sort of just standing in a hallway when someone asked me if I needed help. When I said no, she said OK, and that she had just wanted to make sure I wasn't lost. I told her that was a different issue.

I was lost; I am lost. On the surface, I was lost in thought. More deeply, however, I often feel lost in my own life. This is not a bad thing. Indeed, it has something to do with the sense of awe I experience when I really consider the nature of life and the complexity of human relationships.

A few years ago we were required to develop teaching portfolios and present them to the faculty in our department (mine is available online at markelland.com). I was the first to present my portfolio, and there was one section which I found very interesting as I prepared it: the section on professional development. I realized that my career had involved three distinct stages. First, when I was conducting biomedical research, I became involved in animal care and use issues and the corresponding ethics. I served on the animal care and use committee at the National Institute of Neurological Disorders and Stroke, and I was the first chair of the animal use committee for the International Behavioral Neuroscience Society. I attended conferences on ethics, rules and regulations, accreditation, and relevant laws.

When I went to St. Anselm College, I became active in service-learning. Since teaching was more important than research at this small, 4-year college, it was a natural transition. It allowed me to be an active leader, since service-learning was just taking off as a major trend in education, and I started attending the appropriate conferences. Before long, I was presenting at those conferences, had a small grant to host a seminar, and published a couple of papers on the subject. It was interesting and fun, but a very different direction in my profession.

After coming to LCC, I became interested in Eastern philosophy and religion. I began studying Yoga, Buddhism, and Daoism, as well as incorporating these subjects into my psychology classes. I found that many of my students were very interested, and had some experiences of their own to share.

As I prepared my report on my future career development, I contemplated that I could not possibly have imagined that I would have followed the path I had. So I reported to my colleagues that my plan for future professional development was to have no plan at all. I wasn't being clever, or uncooperative. I realized that I am a very task-oriented person. When I have a clear goal, I pursue it. So if I were to set out a clear plan, I would no longer be open to unexpected possibilities that might arise. And that is exactly what happened.

At that time, I was just becoming interested in martial arts programs for people with physical disabilities. Soon, I applied for a sabbatical leave and it was approved. That gave me the time to study the psychology of disability, Buddhist mindfulness of body, and martial arts programs for people with physical disabilities. I earned black belts in the American Cane System (Cane Masters International Association) and Defense-Ability (International Disabled Self-Defense Association; a program for people who use wheelchairs). I earned certification in the C.R.I.T.I.C.A.L. Approach™ (Natural Motion Martial Arts; a program for instructors teaching martial arts for people with disabilities). I published both an article and a book on the topic. Finally, I started my own business and began working with the Capital Area Business Leadership Network Disability Council in Lansing, MI to set up some programs (this is happening very slowly, but it is moving forward).

As the Buddha taught, attachment leads to suffering. Having specific goals for my career and personal life will be met or not. If not, I would feel bad. If met, I would then need something more, still not being satisfied. So, I am simply doing things, and not concerning myself with the outcome. If I make the world a better place, and myself a better person, that would be nice. But I try not to worry about it.

* * *

80

So, I have great plans for the future. I look forward to helping my children enter adulthood and get a college education. I plan to continue integrating cross-cultural topics into the courses I teach. I will continue training in Brazilian Jiu Jitsu and Muay Thai, lose a few more pounds, get really fit again, and compete in a few more tournaments. And I will try to set a good example for my children and colleagues by developing my program to teach martial arts and self-defense for people with disabilities.

You may have noticed a steady use of the word "I" in the preceding paragraph. Buddhists teach that there is no "I," no self at all. The material world is an illusion, and even as an illusion it is only temporary. I will continue to study Buddhism, as well as Daoism, Yoga, and other spiritual paths. I will meditate, and practice mindfulness. I will strive to fully integrate mindfulness into my life, in the hope that someday there will be no more striving, no more "I." Becoming enlightened is neither an easy nor a simple task, but it is a goal worth pursuing. You just have to realize that there is no goal, and no pursuit, and you don't exist to either have a goal or pursue it.

Actually, I have very strange plans for the future. I hope it proves to be fun. I'm sure it will be interesting. Maybe I'll write a book about how things turn out.

Epilogue

When I told friends what this book was going to be about, it sounded strange even to me. I said it was going to be about how miserable my life has been, and how hopeful I am about the future. This is not something that comes easily. It must be a conscious choice. It requires a great deal of effort, but hopefully the end result will be well worth it. One of the most difficult challenges along the way is to let go of others, even those we love, no matter how much it seems to hurt at the time.

For a second time, I will rely on the words of another to express my feelings:

> The heart in love remains soft and sensitive. But when you're hell-bent on *getting* this or the other thing, you become ruthless, hard, and insensitive. How can you love people when you need people? You can only use them. If I need you to make me happy, I've got to use you, I've got to manipulate you, I've got to find ways and means of winning you. I cannot let you be free. I can only love people when I have emptied my life of people. When I die to the need for people, then I'm right in the desert. In the beginning it feels awful, it feels lonely, but if you can take it for a while, you'll suddenly discover that it isn't lonely at all. It is solitude, it is aloneness, and the desert begins to flower. Then at last you'll know what love is, what God is, what reality is. ... It's a great thing to have suffered. Only then can you get sick of it. You can make use of suffering to end suffering. Most people simply go on suffering. ... Spirituality is awareness, awareness, awareness, ... Nobody does wrong *in awareness...* (pp. 140-142; Anthony de Mello, in *Awareness: The Perils and Opportunities of Reality*, New York, NY: Image Books [1990])

So the path I have chosen for myself is awareness. There are other terms I might use, such as wisdom, or mindfulness, but the words don't really matter. How I live my life is what matters. How I approach each day, how I interact with other people, how I treat my fellow man or woman or child, that is what will determine whether I have become a better person. Becoming a better person is my first goal. Then, I hope to transcend being a person at all, so that I can be one with all those around me, both nearby and far away.

In an odd sense, it is a form of suicide. I hope to destroy the person I was. That person felt he had no place in the world: no family, no friends,

83

no value, no meaning. He was always looking for something, anything, to justify his existence. Just as Gotama Buddha taught us, this led to great suffering, regardless of any objective successes that might have occurred along the path I was following.

The self-less person I hope to become will not be concerned about family. I will let individuals like my children find their own path. I will not be concerned about friends, but I will be a friend to whomever I encounter each day. I will not seek love, but I will make every effort to embody compassion for others, and I will try my best to teach this principle to my students. And just as I now know I often did as a child, I will take walks in the woods and try to mindfully connect with the subtle majesty of this beautiful world we live in.

I will simply *Be*.

Note: *At the beginning of this book I said I wanted to lose 50 pounds. As I send this manuscript to be published, on my lightest day I had dropped from 233 to 192 pounds (a loss of 41 pounds). I put a few pounds back on, but for three months now I have been around 200 pounds, a loss of 30 pounds. I am now going to refocus my efforts to lose the remaining weight (photo courtesy of Megan Ottgen).*

About the Author

Mark Kelland is a Professor of Social Science at Lansing Community College in Michigan. He has a Ph.D. in Physiological Psychology, and for a number of years conducted biomedical research on Parkinson's disease, Tourette syndrome, and schizophrenia. Over time he made a transition to full-time teaching, and now scholarship and writing have taken the place in his career once filled by conducting research.

Prof. Kelland has been active in community service in a variety of ways, including being a volunteer reader at several schools, tutoring first-graders in reading, teaching religious education, and serving as a coach in youth soccer programs. He was a founding faculty member of the Adult Center for Enrichment of Livingston County (Michigan), and has offered classes on psychology, spirituality, and self-defense at the Hartland Senior Center and the Howell Parks & Recreation Department. He has been a member of the Capital Area Business Leadership Network Disability Council in Lansing, MI, and recently he was one of the readers at the Cromaine Library (Hartland, MI) Banned Books Read-Out.

Physically active throughout his life, including nine years in the U. S. Marine Corps Reserve, Prof. Kelland did not begin formal martial arts training until his mid-40s. By the time he was 50 years old he had earned a black belt in Taekwondo, and had both hips replaced (due to an old injury). He began to study martial arts programs for people with physical disabilities, and earned black belts in both the American Cane System and Defense-Ability (for people who use a wheelchair). He also earned certification in the C.R.I.T.I.C.A.L. Approach™ to teaching martial arts to people with disabilities

Currently, Prof. Kelland trains in Brazilian Jiu Jitsu and Muay Thai at Magic BJJ in E. Lansing, MI. He has taught self-defense courses through his own company, Real-Life Self-Defense, LLC, and is currently teaching Defense-Ability at Magic BJJ and a meditation class at the Hartland (MI) Senior Center.

Books by Mark Kelland

Personality Theory in a Cultural Context

Psychological and Spiritual Factors in Martial Arts Programs for People with Physical Disabilities

Two Months of Magic

Made in the USA
Lexington, KY
16 August 2011